WHAT YOUR COLLEAGUES ARE SAYING . . .

"Too often, middle school and high school teachers say, 'These students are lacking number sense.' These books will help secondary teachers with good pedagogy to help build number sense in a creative way. Eric and John have created short routines that are teacher-friendly with lots of examples and easy to adapt to each teacher's needs. These are the books that secondary teachers have been waiting for to help engage students in building number sense."

—Pamela J. Dombrowski
Secondary Math Specialist
Geary County School District
Junction City, KS

"Thank you, Eric and John, for creating this practical resource that supports and guides high school mathematics teachers in redesigning beginnings of mathematics lessons to capture attention and engage ALL students in mathematical reasoning, mental mathematics, and discourse in order to develop deeper understandings of number and improve overall mathematics learning. This book is a necessary resource for EVERY high school mathematics teacher!"

—Becky Walker
Director of Learning
Wisconsin Mathematics Learning
Appleton, WI

"'Routines' in the high school classrooms are needed to help transform instructional practices that start classes with meaningful engagement opportunities and connect to students' previous learned practices from elementary and middle school mathematics classrooms."

—John W. Staley
Director of Mathematics PreK–12
Baltimore County Public Schools
Baltimore, MD

"Don't just manipulate symbols, help students ponder about what the symbols mean. This book provides effective ways of helping students stretch the limits of their thinking and develop a deeper understanding of mathematics. It can really help in achieving your primary goal—the development of developing comfortable and confident problem solvers!"

—Jim Rubillo
Executive Director (2001–2009)
National Council of Teachers of Mathematics

Daily Routines to Jump-Start Math Class, High School

THE BOOK AT-A-GLANCE

A quick-reference table provides you with a brief description of each routine, along with the corresponding purpose.

JUMP-START ROUTINES AT-A-GLANCE

	ROUTINE	DESCRIPTION	PURPOSE
1	Missing Numbers	Students consider open problems where some of the numbers are missing.	Develop reasoning about skills and concepts by considering multiple possibilities when numbers are missing in a problem.
2	Order Me on the Number Line	Students use a number line (or double number line) representation to develop thinking and reasoning about numbers, variables, and relationships.	Determine viable options for numbers or variables on a number line, and examine the relationship between such.
3	More or Less?	Students compare expressions to a known value.	Reinforce computational fluency and reasoning by estimating and determining reasonable answers by comparing estimates to a given benchmark.
4	Two Wrongs and a Right	Students consider the accuracy of different solutions.	Develop reasoning about skills and concepts by considering multiple possibilities.
5	A or B	Students compare two different quantities and determine if they are equal, if one is larger than the other, or if inadequate information is provided to make the determination.	Reason quickly and accurately about the relative sizes of two quantities, engage in logical and numerical analysis, and perceive that, in some cases, not enough information is provided to make such a decision.

Video Demonstrations bring the jump-start routines to life and help you visualize how they might work in your classroom.

JUMP-START ROUTINES

VIDEO DEMONSTRATIONS:

- Missing Numbers, **Example 1**
- Missing Numbers, **Example 2**
- Order Me on the Number Line, **Example 1**
- Order Me on the Number Line, **Example 2**
- Order Me on the Number Line, **Example 3**
- More or Less? **Example 1**
- More or Less? **Example 2**
- More or Less? **Example 3**
- Two Wrongs and a Right, **Example 1**
- Two Wrongs and a Right, **Example 2**
- Two Wrongs and a Right, **Example 3**
- A or B

online resources All videos can be viewed at resources.corwin.com/jumpstartroutines/highschool

An **About the Routine** section provides an overview of what the routine entails.

Why It Matters sections encapsulate the relevance of the routine for student learning and call out any related Standards for Mathematical Practice.

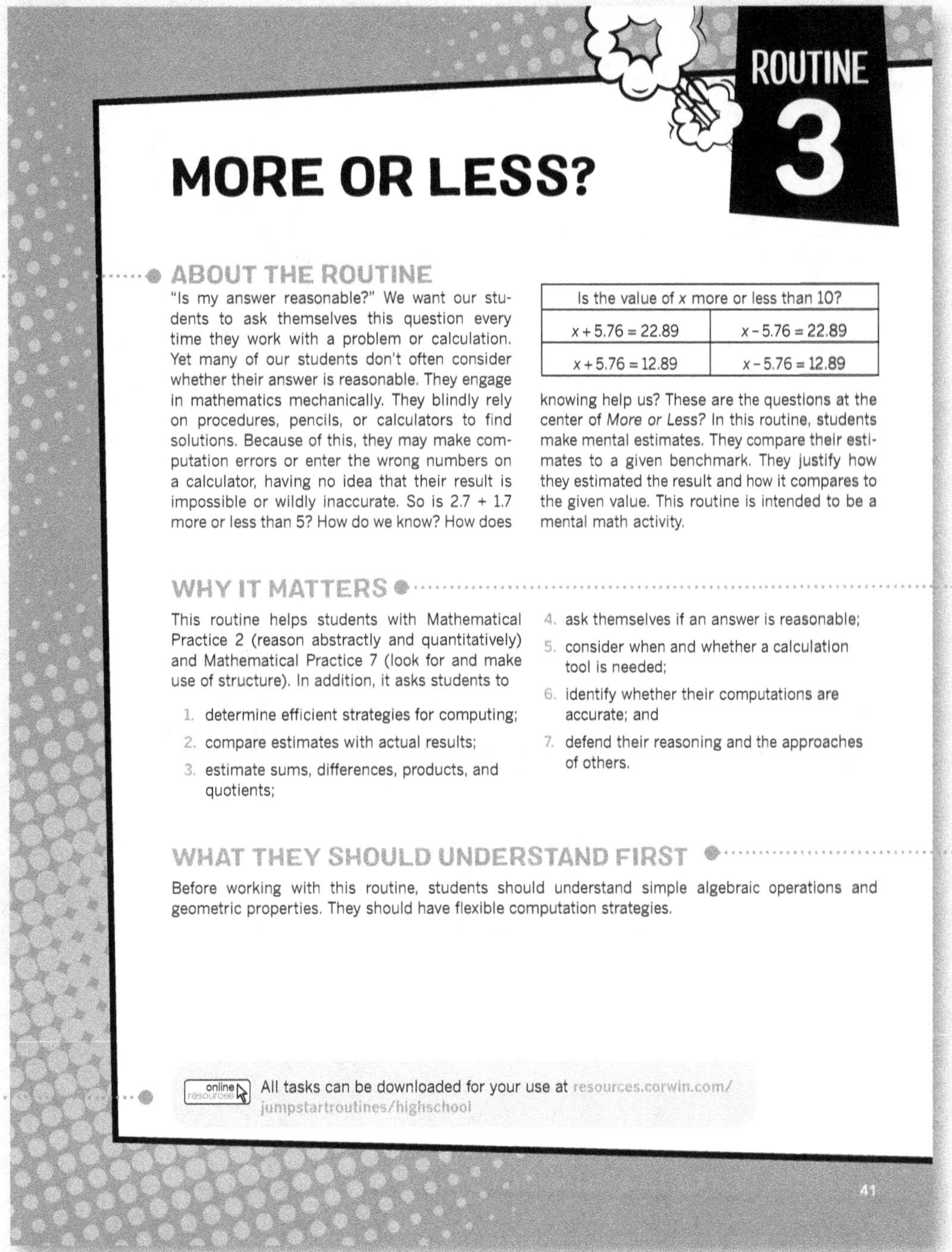

ROUTINE 3

MORE OR LESS?

ABOUT THE ROUTINE

"Is my answer reasonable?" We want our students to ask themselves this question every time they work with a problem or calculation. Yet many of our students don't often consider whether their answer is reasonable. They engage in mathematics mechanically. They blindly rely on procedures, pencils, or calculators to find solutions. Because of this, they may make computation errors or enter the wrong numbers on a calculator, having no idea that their result is impossible or wildly inaccurate. So is 2.7 + 1.7 more or less than 5? How do we know? How does knowing help us? These are the questions at the center of *More or Less?* In this routine, students make mental estimates. They compare their estimates to a given benchmark. They justify how they estimated the result and how it compares to the given value. This routine is intended to be a mental math activity.

Is the value of x more or less than 10?	
$x + 5.76 = 22.89$	$x - 5.76 = 22.89$
$x + 5.76 = 12.89$	$x - 5.76 = 12.89$

WHY IT MATTERS

This routine helps students with Mathematical Practice 2 (reason abstractly and quantitatively) and Mathematical Practice 7 (look for and make use of structure). In addition, it asks students to

1. determine efficient strategies for computing;
2. compare estimates with actual results;
3. estimate sums, differences, products, and quotients;
4. ask themselves if an answer is reasonable;
5. consider when and whether a calculation tool is needed;
6. identify whether their computations are accurate; and
7. defend their reasoning and the approaches of others.

WHAT THEY SHOULD UNDERSTAND FIRST

Before working with this routine, students should understand simple algebraic operations and geometric properties. They should have flexible computation strategies.

online resources All tasks can be downloaded for your use at resources.corwin.com/jumpstartroutines/highschool

41

Online Resources icons signal the availability of downloadable tasks.

What They Should Understand First sections explain what mathematics students should ideally know before embarking on the routine at hand.

What to Do sections break down exactly how to use the routine in your classroom, step by step.

WHAT TO DO

1. Present a few expressions, equations, or graphs to students.
2. Have them decide how the results will compare to a given benchmark. As noted, this is a mental mathematics opportunity. Students should not use tools to find exact values.
3. Provide time for students to reason.
4. Have students share their ideas with a partner before having a whole-class discussion.
5. Begin the whole-class discussion by identifying who believed which of the choices met the benchmark question.
6. Ask students to share how they made their decisions. As students share their thinking, it is important to probe thinking and ask clarifying questions rather than ask questions to establish how they thought about the expression. Here are some questions you might ask:
   - How did you estimate your solution?
   - Might there have been a more precise estimate?
   - Did you approach the expression in a different way?
   - How are different strategies similar?
7. Honor and explore both accurate and flawed reasoning.
8. Consider providing exact values after discussion so that students can compare and confirm their more or less estimates.

ANTICIPATED STRATEGIES FOR THIS EXAMPLE

Our students can and should reason about the value of a variable in equations. But they often go about solving equations by "doing to one side what is done to the other." And, as we know, the process can unravel quickly. But what if our students paused to consider whether an equation is simplistic enough to solve mentally? What if they were empowered to solve it without using paper and pencil? What if they reasoned about what the value of a variable might be before solving for it?

Students can approach each equation in various ways. Some students will consistently substitute the given value for the variable to make sense of what the true value might be. Some will consistently solve and compare the results. And some will guess and check possible solutions that they will then compare to the given value. There is nothing wrong with a preferred strategy. However, exposure to the strategies of others may help individuals refine their ideas about efficiency.

Is the value of x more or less than 10?	
$x+5.76=22.89$	$x-5.76=22.89$
$x+5.76=12.89$	$x-5.76=12.89$

In this example, strange unwieldy decimals are present in the equations to push students away from calculating toward mental mathematics.

- The top left (referred to as A) must be larger than 10 as 10 + 5.76 is not large enough to equal 22.89.
- The top right (referred to as B) must be larger than 10 as 10 − 5.76 is not large enough to equal 22.89. In fact, the answer to B is larger than the answer to A.
- The bottom left (referred to as C) is less than 10 as 10 + 5.76 would be greater than 12.89.
- The bottom right (referred to as D) is greater than 10 as 10 − 5.76 would be much smaller than 12.89.

Anticipated Strategies for This Example sections describe and distill the key strategies that will likely arise while students are working through each routine.

ALGEBRA GEOMETRY DATA ANALYSIS

ADDITIONAL EXAMPLES

Additional Examples sections explain how you can adjust the routine and leverage it to further develop students' mathematical skills.

ALGEBRA

In examples 1 to 19, the content is from the algebra curriculum. It is often the case that students do not have to actually calculate or compute the missing variable or information but can use algebraic reasoning and relationships to determine the solution to the example. Be mindful of this when listening to students' solutions.

1

Is the value of x greater or less than 0?

$3.2x - 17.8 = 0$	$3.2x + 17.8 = 0$
$3.2x - 17.8 = 0$	$-3.2x - 17.8 = 0$

1. Students should not actually solve these equations, merely moving the constant term to the right-hand side of the equation and then examining the signs of the coefficient of x and the constant term. In the top-left equation, $3.2x = 17.8$, since both the coefficient of x and the constant term are positive, the solution will be positive.

A) Top left: $x > 0$

B) Top right: $x < 0$

C) Bottom left: $x < 0$

D) Bottom right: $x > 0$

ALGEBRA GEOMETRY DATA ANALYSIS

Each **Additional Examples** section includes examples from Algebra and at least one other branch of mathematics.

GEOMETRY

The next set of examples (20–27) reviews some basic areas of geometry including area, perimeter, volume, parallel lines, and right angle trigonometry. You might decide to provide the necessary formulas for your students when they are solving the examples.

20

Is the area of the circle greater or less than π?

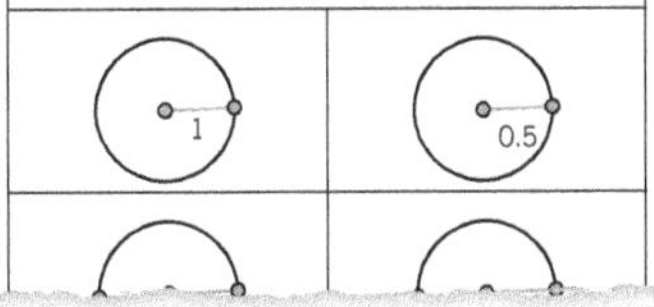

20. Since the area of a circle is πr^2, to see if the area > π, students need to determine only whether the radius^2 > 1.

A) Top left: radius^2 = 1, area = π

B) Top right: radius^2 < 1, area < π

C) Bottom left: radius^2 > 1, area > π

D) Bottom right: radius^2 < 1, area < π

ALGEBRA GEOMETRY DATA ANALYSIS

For easy navigation, a tab at the top of each page highlights the relevant subsection within the **Additional Examples**.

DATA ANALYSIS

The last three examples (28–30) involve basic probability and data analysis.

28

When rolling a single die, is the probability of the event greater or less than $\frac{1}{2}$?

Prime number	Number > 4
Number with more than 2 factors	Odd number > 1

28. Students should quickly note that the sample space = {1, 2, 3, 4, 5, 6}.

A) Top left: {2, 3, 5}, probability = $\frac{1}{2}$

B) Top right: {5, 6}, probability < $\frac{1}{2}$

C) Bottom left: {4, 6}, probability < $\frac{1}{2}$

D) Bottom right: {3, 5}, probability < $\frac{1}{2}$

29

Is the mean of the given set of numbers greater or less than 10?

29. There is no need to actually compute the mean of the data sets here. Students should use mental mathematics to think about how far the data points are from 10 in either direction.

A) Top left: mean > 10

DAILY ROUTINES to JUMP-START MATH CLASS

HIGH SCHOOL

DAILY ROUTINES to JUMP-START MATH CLASS

HIGH SCHOOL

Engage Students, Improve Number Sense, and Practice Reasoning

ERIC
MILOU

JOHN J.
SANGIOVANNI

CM CORWIN MATHEMATICS

CORWIN
A SAGE Publishing Company

FOR INFORMATION:

Corwin
A SAGE Company
2455 Teller Road
Thousand Oaks, California 91320
(800) 233–9936
www.corwin.com

SAGE Publications Ltd.
1 Oliver's Yard
55 City Road
London, EC1Y 1SP
United Kingdom

SAGE Publications India Pvt. Ltd.
B 1/I 1 Mohan Cooperative Industrial Area
Mathura Road, New Delhi 110 044
India

SAGE Publications Asia-Pacific Pte. Ltd.
3 Church Street
#10–04 Samsung Hub
Singapore 049483

Program Manager, Mathematics: Erin Null
Associate Editor: Julie Nemer
Editorial Assistant: Jessica Vidal
Production Editor: Tori Mirsadjadi
Copy Editor: Sarah J. Duffy
Typesetter: Integra
Proofreader: Scott Oney
Cover and Interior Designer: Scott Van Atta
Marketing Manager: Margaret O'Connor

Library of Congress Cataloging-in-Publication Data

Names: Milou, Eric, author. | SanGiovanni, John, author.

Title: Daily routines to jump-start math class—high school : engage students, improve number sense, and practice reasoning/Eric Milou and John J. SanGiovanni.

Description: Thousand Oaks, California: Corwin, 2019. | Includes bibliographical references and index.

Identifiers: LCCN 2018008911 | ISBN 9781544316932 (pbk.)

Subjects: LCSH: Mathematics—Study and teaching (Secondary)
Classification: LCC QA11.2 .M556 2018 | DDC 510.71/2—dc23 LC record available at https://lccn.loc.gov/2018008911

18 19 20 21 22 10 9 8 7 6 5 4 3 2 1

CONTENTS

Note From the Publisher: The authors have provided video and web content throughout the book that is available to you through QR (quick response) codes. To read a QR code, you must have a smartphone or tablet with a camera. We recommend that you download a QR code reader app that is made specifically for your phone or tablet brand.
Videos may also be accessed at **resources.corwin.com/jumpstartroutines/highschool**.

ACKNOWLEDGMENTS

This book has been a collaborative effort. We are grateful to Corwin for making this project a reality. We are thankful that they recognize the importance of reasoning, number sense, computational fluency, discussion, and student engagement. We appreciate that they, too, know that we can develop these in our students through brief, engaging activities that are practical and doable for incredibly busy teachers.

We would like to especially thank the following teachers, coaches, and administrators who embody the best of mathematics education. Thank you to the staff at Middletown Township School District and Middletown High School in New Jersey. They welcomed us into their classrooms to record these jump-start routines in action. These brief videos help bring the activities to life and help readers better understand how to implement them in their classrooms. Those individuals are Marjorie M. Caruso, John Kerrigan, Matt Martone, Kara Teehan, Paige Friedland, and their students.

Thanks to our many other "math friends" who make us better. They listen, question, and inspire.

Thanks to the staff at Corwin for transforming a featureless document into such an appealing, practical tool for teaching and learning. Special thanks to Erin Null for her enthusiasm, partnership, thoughtful questions, and insight.

Lastly and most importantly, many thanks to our families. We cannot thank them enough for their endless support and encouragement.

PUBLISHER'S ACKNOWLEDGMENTS

Corwin gratefully acknowledges the contributions of the following reviewers:

Cathy Battles
Consultant
UMKC Regional Professional Development Center
Kansas City, MO

John W. Staley
Director of Mathematics PreK–12
Baltimore County Public Schools
Baltimore, MD

Michele Mailhot
Mathematics Specialist
Independent Contractor
Oakland, ME

Marissa Walsh
Math Instructional Coach
Blue Springs School District
Blue Springs, MO

Pamela J. Dombrowski
Secondary Math Specialist
Greary County School District USD 475
Greary County, KS

Michelle Parks
Math Consultant
Cooperative Education Service Agency #10
Chippewa Falls, WI

Brian Shay
Teacher and Department Chair
Canyon Crest Academy, San Dieguito Union High School
San Diego, CA

Crystal Steinmetz
Director of Curriculum and Instruction
Garden City Public School USD #457
Garden City, KS

Becky Walker
Director of Learning
Wisconsin Mathematics Learning
Green Bay, WI

ABOUT THE AUTHORS

Eric Milou is a professor of mathematics at Rowan University in Glassboro, New Jersey. Dr. Milou has taught at Rowan for the past 20 years and served six terms as the president of the Rowan University Senate from 2007 to 2013. He previously served as president of the Association of Mathematics Teachers of New Jersey and the program chairperson of the 2007 National Council of Teachers of Mathematics annual meeting. He has extensive speaking experience on standards-based reform in mathematics. He is one of the authors of *digits, EnVisions 6–8,* and *EnVisions A|G|A* (published by Pearson) and was the recipient of the Max Sobel Outstanding Mathematics Educator Award in 2009.

John J. SanGiovanni is a mathematics supervisor in Howard County, Maryland. There he leads mathematics curriculum development, digital learning, assessment, and professional development for 41 elementary schools and more than 1,500 teachers. John is an adjunct professor and coordinator of the Elementary Mathematics Instructional Leader graduate program at McDaniel College. He is an author and national mathematics curriculum and professional learning consultant. John is a frequent speaker at national conferences and institutes. He is active in state and national professional organizations and currently serves on the Board of Directors for the National Council of Teachers of Mathematics.

PART 1

WHY JUMP-START ROUTINES?

THE FIRST FEW MINUTES OF MATHEMATICS CLASS

The opening few minutes of a mathematics class offer a rich opportunity to capture the attention of students and prepare them for the lesson ahead. As teachers, we must be aware, however, that students often walk into our classes with all of the distractions of their electronic lives as well as issues with friends, parents, or even health concerns. Their bodies may be in a room with us for the required time period, but their minds may be somewhere else entirely. The opening minutes are also the time when students' brains are freshest and they tend to remember more of what is being taught during this segment than at any other time during the learning episode (Sousa, 2007). That is why it is such a critical time to help students shed their distractions, capture their attention, and jump-start their brains. Engaging students immediately increases the likelihood that they'll stay engaged and motivated to learn throughout the lesson.

Why the Traditional Warm-Up Doesn't Work

Many times, the first 5 minutes of class are spent on logistical or low-level cognitive tasks such as taking attendance, reviewing homework, or completing problems that are identical to homework problems assigned the night before. While the goal may be to tap into prior learning, such problems are usually rote in nature and ask students to perform simple tasks that often stress procedure and "correctness."

Positioning warm-ups like these as the first "instructional" tasks presents challenges. It signals to students that mathematics is the pursuit of low-level answers and procedures. It suggests that mathematics is a collection of semiconnected ideas and steps. Students may infer that you value these sorts of problems more than others. These problems might tell your students that you need them to consistently review ideas because you aren't confident or convinced that they have mastered the skills within them. Such warm-ups may fail to take advantage of the moments in which your students' brains are most ready to learn. The most problematic aspect of these warm-ups may be that they fail to set the stage for engagement and discussion.

We know from experience that great lessons begin with a strong start. Many, if not all, of us would agree that the opening minutes of class have the potential to ignite engagement and take advantage of our students' brains being ready to learn. Conversely, a start to class that drags or is uninteresting can sabotage the rest of the period. The traditional warm-up often sets the stage for the latter. But what if it didn't?

The Problem With Going Over Homework

Research on the effectiveness of homework suggests that doing homework *can* improve academic achievement for high school students. However, according to two studies of secondary school mathematics classrooms, 15 to 20 percent of class time tends to be spent reviewing homework (Grouws, Tarr, Sears, & Ross, 2010; Otten, Herbel-Eisenmann, & Cirillo, 2012). We fundamentally believe that reviewing homework for any significant amount of time in class is an ineffective way to begin class.

For many teachers, reviewing homework is an unwritten obligation for planning mathematics class. It is where math should start or something that should be done after a warm-up. But it is not a requirement for effective mathematics instruction. In fact, it can contribute to the opposite of effective mathematics instruction. So why is going over homework problematic?

First, remember the intended purpose of homework. Homework should be designed and used for practice of previously learned skills and concepts that students are able to complete independently. Unfortunately, we often see homework becoming the fulfillment of a lesson that a teacher was unable to complete in class. Not only does that unfairly put the burden of independent learning on students, but the teacher is then in the position of reviewing and grading work that students have to complete without enough knowledge. This usually results in follow-up instructional time needed to troubleshoot and clarify. It can also create a culture of assessment based on minimal or incomplete teaching.

Second, even if homework is set to practice skills taught completely that particular day, specific items within a homework assignment can sometimes be problematic. These items may be uniquely complicated or simply missed by everyone in the class. As the teacher then explores these items, it suddenly becomes necessary to conduct an ad hoc mini-lesson, to clarify something that was really a weakness in the assignment itself. In no time, significant instructional time has been lost, regardless of students' performance or understanding.

Third, and just as important, even having students complete and turn in their homework can be a problem. Some students forget their homework. Others are unable or choose not to do it because of circumstances at home. Incompleteness of homework means that class time dedicated to reviewing it is already compromised. And even those who complete it may not have done so independently as some students have better access to support. These students may have no better understanding than their classmates but their "work" shows otherwise.

The bottom line is that if homework is used appropriately to reinforce existing knowledge and help students keep skills fresh, then it shouldn't need much, if any, class time for review. Instead, we propose using that time more productively. Starting math class with number sense and reasoning routines that can engage students and foster their curiosity and creative thinking immediately will allow you to take back the time lost to rote warm-ups and review of homework.

JUMP-START ROUTINES: NEW WARM-UPS FOR A NEW ERA

The routines in this book are designed to jump-start mathematics class. They are new warm-ups for a new era. They are engaging opportunities for students to work with and discuss interesting prompts. The routines are designed to develop students' reasoning, critical thinking, and/or sense making. They aim to improve students' number sense. They are a makeover for the beginning of class as they replace traditional warm-ups and homework review with meaningful, engaging, quality practice. These routines can repair or instill mathematics confidence in our students.

These routines are

- practical and easy for teachers to implement each day,
- meant for the first 5 minutes of class,
- thinking exercises designed to ignite thinking and reasoning skills,
- open and flexible in nature, and
- modifiable to work with almost any content.

These routines create an environment in which the Common Core State Standards for mathematics (Governors Association Center for Best Practices & Council of Chief State School Officers, 2010) come to life. Though specific practices are linked to each routine throughout the book, in general students

1. make sense of problems and persevere in solving them,
2. reason abstractly and quantitatively,
3. construct viable arguments and critique the reasoning of others,
4. model with mathematics,
5. use appropriate tools strategically,
6. attend to precision,
7. look for and make use of structure, and
8. look for and express regularity in repeated reasoning.

Concretely, these routines are designed to get students reasoning and thinking. Specifically, they help students

- enhance their ability to determine reasonableness of answers or solutions;
- examine errors in given problems, explaining what's wrong and why;
- reason metacognitively about the *strategies* that they are using; and
- communicate their solutions and reasoning to others.

Routines for Reasoning in Mathematics

You can think of reasoning as the process of drawing conclusions based on evidence or stated assumptions. Although reasoning is an important part of all disciplines, it plays a special and fundamental role in mathematics. In secondary school mathematics, reasoning is often understood as engaging in *formal reasoning*, or formulating proofs, in which students draw conclusions logically deduced from assumptions and definitions. However, mathematical reasoning can take many forms, ranging from informal explanation and justification to formal deduction as well as inductive observations. Reasoning often begins with explorations, conjectures at various levels, false starts, and partial explanations before there is ever a result. As students develop a repertoire of increasingly sophisticated methods of reasoning and proof during their time in high school, "standards for accepting explanations should become more stringent" (National Council of Teachers of Mathematics, 2000, p. 342).

Yet reasoning is compromised as students accept rule and procedure without investigation of *why*. They then practice these rules and procedures so much so that the mathematics and reasoning within them fades away. Their task at hand becomes nothing more than completing a collection of problems. Over time, they generalize that this is what it means to do mathematics.

Today, technology makes it possible to solve or complete almost any calculation quickly. But how do students know that the result is reasonable? How do they know that a solution displayed on a calculator or monitor is correct? Determining reasonableness is a collection of abilities and skills, which are much different from procedural calculation. These skills include critical thinking, reasoning, problem solving, and communicating. In fact, these more complex skills are more desired by Fortune 500 companies than those skills, such as calculation, that were once considered desirable (Boaler, 2015a).

The routines proposed here help students develop complex, essential skills through daily, engaging activities that represent quality practice. The strategies, approaches, and reasoning that they develop during these routines will serve them for a lifetime of everyday mathematics.

Routines for Improving Number Sense and Reasoning

The National Council of Teachers of Mathematics (1999) identifies five components of number sense: number meaning, number relationships, number magnitude, operations involving numbers, and referents for numbers and quantities. Fennell and Landis (1994) describe number sense as "an awareness and understanding about what numbers are, their relationships, their magnitude, the relative effect of operating on numbers, including the use of mental mathematics and estimation" (p. 187). Students with number sense understand relationships between numbers. They estimate. They make use of the properties of operations. They manipulate. Fennell and Landis also describe number sense as "the foundation from which all other mathematical concepts and ideas arise" (p. 188). And every mathematics teacher relates to their noting that "students with number sense show a good intuition about numbers and their relationships" (p. 187).

There is likely no correlation between the number of problems on a page and the level of one's number sense or reasoning. Students don't develop these skills by completing a certain quantity of problems. Instead, you can help your students develop them through rich, engaging problems and tasks, through exposure to others' sense and reasoning, and with sound understanding and lots of opportunity for meaningful practice. Routines can be part of that opportunity.

Number sense and reasoning extend far beyond whole numbers and basic facts to fractions, decimals, ratios, percentages, and much more. Most, if not all, mathematics teachers would identify number sense and reasoning as two of the things that matter most. They might also identify them as two of the biggest challenges their students face in mathematics. Because of this, number sense and reasoning are the targets of every routine in this book.

10,000 Hours of Practice

In his book *Outliers*, Malcolm Gladwell (2008) suggests that a person needs 10,000 hours of deliberate practice to master something. Though one might argue the exact amount of time, it is logical that the more people do something—the more they practice and experience something—the better they can understand and apply it. Take for example driving a car. Passing a written driver's exam doesn't mean someone is a proficient driver. Instead, it shows that they understand the rules of the road and the basics of how a car operates. Their ability to drive a car well is improved and enhanced as they do it more and more.

This analogy could be applied to number sense and reasoning. The theory here is that with foundational understanding and frequent, plentiful opportunities to practice, students can develop a noticeable sense of number, reasoning, and justification. You might note that 10,000 hours seems impossible with limited instructional time and considerable skills and concepts already identified in your curriculum. However, with routines such as those presented in this book, your students can achieve a grand amount of "hours on the road" in just a few minutes a day. Consider this: your students could access 11,700 minutes of number sense practice through 5 minutes a day, for 180 days (in a school year), over a 13-year school career. That's 195 hours—or more than one instructional year—for just number sense and reasoning!

Routines That Satisfy the Need for Quality Practice

Quality practice is not defined by the number of problems students complete, the speed at which they calculate, nor the number of hours they spend doing mathematics. It is defined by what students do and how they are engaged. Quality practice should engage students in thinking. We mean for the routines in this book to provide quality practice. They offer distinctive, engaging, and diverse experiences that will help students develop their thinking skills. They are not repetitive nor mundane. They are not mindless drills. These routines provide the quality practice that can help our students perform better in class, outside the mathematics classroom, and even on standardized tests.

Routines for Achieving Improved Performance

Data from 13 million students who took PISA tests showed that the lowest achieving students worldwide were those who used a memorization strategy (Boaler, 2015). Simply put, thinking and making connections improves students' success on standardized tests. Mental computation and estimation can improve students' speed and overall performance. This makes most sense when we consider that test makers design distractors to mimic students' most common computational errors. It makes sense that students who estimate, discount possibilities, and make decisions about reasonable answers will reconsider their solutions when choices don't match solutions. Routines that develop reasoning and number sense help students gain confidence, practice thinking, and likely improve overall performance on standardized assessments.

Routines for Rehabilitating Number Pluckers, Pluggers, and Crunchers

One might say that traditional mathematics instruction has created a bunch of "pluckers": students who pluck key words or numbers from problems without thinking. It has created "pluggers" who plug numbers into formulas and equations without thinking. It has created "crunchers" who crunch numbers and blindly rely on the results as being correct. The creation of these pluckers, pluggers, and crunchers doesn't happen by accident. It can be the result of students who perceive mathematics to be a collection of procedures or the pursuit of answers.

Success can be fleeting for many, if not all, of our pluckers, pluggers, and crunchers. Their ability to complete a procedure with understanding can, and often is, lost without considerable practice and maintenance. Even then, proficiency can fade. Yet understanding is not lost. When students understand concepts, connect them to procedures, refine their understanding, and transfer it to new situations, they show that they never lose it. Routines build on their conceptual understanding and allow students to connect ideas, refine them, and transfer them to new situations. Routines build number sense and fluency. Routines can rehabilitate these students so that they rely on their own thinking instead of or in addition to someone else's rules and procedures.

Routines for a Growth Mindset

The idea of consistent, engaging practice to develop your students' number sense and reasoning promotes other prominent ideas about teaching and learning. One of those is a growth mindset. A growth mindset is an approach to teaching mathematics that emphasizes that mindset is more important than initial ability in determining the progress students can make in their mathematical understanding. Students with a growth mindset make better progress than those with a fixed mindset. Having a growth mindset means

- believing that talents can be developed and great abilities can be built over time,
- viewing mistakes as an opportunity to develop understanding,
- being resilient,
- believing that effort creates success, and
- thinking about how one learns.

Carol Dweck's (2006) work establishes that a growth mindset benefits students by empowering them to develop skills through dedication and hard work. For this to happen, you must provide them with worthwhile opportunities to engage in and discuss reasoning. Daily routines to work with interesting activities, to build number sense, and to improve reasoning about number and operation naturally complement the facets of a growth mindset. Routines reinforce that students' ability can be developed through continued practice and effort. They help students build confidence. They can undermine any students' notion that their mathematics ability is fixed.

Routines to Honor and Leverage Errors

A growth mindset is grounded in making and honoring mistakes. Honoring mistakes is much more than saying that it's OK to make a mistake in class. Honoring mistakes means that you also explore mistakes and consider why they happened. As Boaler (2015a) notes, mistakes help grow our brains. Routines are an opportunity for students to reason and make mistakes when doing so. Discussion about reasoning and mistakes helps students advance their understanding. As you facilitate discussions during routines, it is critical to pursue not only accurate and efficient reasoning but flawed reasoning as well. Exploring their reasoning and errors tells your students more than the fact that mistakes are OK. It tells them that you value mistakes.

As we know, it is more powerful to find our own mistake rather than being told that we are incorrect. During discussion with partners and the class as a whole, students have the opportunity to explain their thinking and thus catch their own mistake. In some cases, exposure to others' reasoning and even others' errors helps students better understand their own reasoning and misconceptions. This can happen at any point during a math class. Starting with a routine built on reasoning and discussion increases, if not guarantees, the likelihood of discussion and exploration of errors or misconceptions.

Routines to Actively Develop Confidence

Blindly applying rules to mathematics without understanding can undermine students' confidence as they rely on disconnected steps without understanding (Van de Walle, Karp, & Bay-Williams, 2010). Stalled fluency erodes confidence. Perceptions of failure associated with making mistakes in mathematics or perceptions of "not having a math gene" damage students' confidence. Infrequent, disengaging, or disconnected practice challenges confidence. Yet jump-start routines can counter each of these challenges and in time enhance your students' confidence in themselves and in mathematics in general.

IMPLEMENTING JUMP-START ROUTINES

These routines are intended as practical ideas for jump-starting your mathematics class. They can be modified to work with any number concept and almost any mathematics concept in general. They can be adjusted to any amount of time allocated to begin mathematics class. They can be used with any level of student proficiency in mathematics and any level of student experience with routines. As they are implemented, routines become a rich opportunity for meaningful discourse in mathematics and windows into student thinking.

online resources All tasks can be downloaded for your use at resources.corwin.com/jumpstartroutines/highschool.

Routines That Are Ready for Use

The routines provided throughout this book are ready for use. Each routine is available as a downloadable set of PowerPoint slides. Each can be edited or modified as needed for any classroom. You can modify the slides to extend a routine to different types of numbers or concepts. Specific numbers, operations, or concepts are provided as examples of how a routine may be used. And additional examples are provided to give ideas about how the content might be modified.

Also, to help you get started, these routines have been recorded in real classrooms. The videos give you a sense of the timing for the routine. They provide insight into how students might reason about certain situations. They help you think about the questions you might ask your students during the routine. Seeing these routines in action can help you develop an understanding of how you might use them in your classroom. You can access these videos at **resources.corwin.com/jumpstartroutines/highschool**.

Flexible Use

We intend for the routines presented here to support high-quality mathematics instruction. There are no specific requirements. You can adjust the time allotted to a routine for all sorts of needs. You can adjust the number of prompts. You can use any routine, in any order, on any day. We offer ideas for using and adjusting routines throughout this book, but there are likely many other ways to adjust them. You can modify any routine however you see fit.

Timing of Routines: How Long? When?

You can manage how long routines last by adjusting the number of questions you ask or the number of student approaches you investigate. You can limit the number of problems or situations that students encounter. You can modify the complexity of the mathematics you present. You can cut or extend the amount of time students have to share their thinking with partners. Essentially, you control the amount of time allocated to your routine. Here is one guide for facilitating a routine:

- Students work with the prompt independently (about 1 minute).
- Students discuss their reasoning in a pair or triad (about 2 minutes).
- Teacher facilitates class discussion about strategies and reasoning (about 2 minutes).

That said, here are a couple of basic guidelines:

1. These routines are intended to be quick, engaging activities that foster number sense and reasoning. Typically, they should be no more than 5 minutes. Occasionally, the discussion may be so vibrant and engaging that you find your class spending 19 minutes with the routine. The latter may not be ideal due to time and schedule challenges, but it's important to note that it may happen from time to time. It's also important to note that these rich discussions are exactly what you want for your students, so spending a few minutes more with them shouldn't be thought of as time lost or wasted.
2. We think these routines are best situated at the beginning of the mathematics class. You can establish protocols for students to enter class and prepare for the opening routine. In this way, they naturally replace mundane warm-ups or

review of homework. However, you can flexibly position routines throughout the class as well. In longer block classes, you may decide that they are best used in the middle of the block as an opportunity for rekindling students' energy and engagement. In other cases, you may find that routines can be useful when offered at the end of the class. If you select the end of class, you must be sure to close instruction for the period early enough for the routine to take place. There is the obvious challenge of running out of time when planning for routines at the end of class.

Which Routines to Use?

We offer a selection of varied routines for use in the classroom. There is no suggestion of which to use, when to use them, or how to order the routines. There is no requirement for length of use or timing within the quarter or semester. The recommendation is to use routines that are most comfortable to facilitate and most interesting for your students to investigate. You should select a routine and use it for a few days or weeks before moving on to another. You may circle back to the first routine after students have experienced other routines. It's important to remember that any routine can become stale with too much use. You can make subtle adjustments to the routine to keep it fresh. Even so, it will be wise to change out routines as needed.

PLAN FOR THE ROUTINE

While you should focus most of your planning energy on the core skills and concepts of the main lesson, you can incorporate short warm-up routines easily because they are designed for low-intensity planning. They are designed to be replicated with minimal change to develop student number sense and reasoning. You should be able to change out skills and concepts within the routine with little effort. However, there are some things to keep in mind when selecting and planning the routine.

Select the Routine and the Content or Concepts

Obviously, you need to know how to facilitate the routine. You must understand the basic tenets of the routine. You must also select skills and concepts that are appropriate for your students. You must decide whether you want to feature algebra or geometry. You need to determine whether your students need help with operational sense or more general number sense. Experience will tell you this, but you also might take cues from class discussion, student work, or test results about what topics and ideas you need to develop with your students. Armed with this information, you can prepare the routine.

The routine content draws mainly from algebra and geometry as these are the crucial content areas that all high school students must master. Students in these classes can use these routines to help with the content they are learning. Students in other classes such as Algebra II or Statistics could use these routines to brush up on prior content.

Use Routines to Set the Stage for Meaningful Discourse

Because discussion is such a critical component of the routines in this book, Smith and Stein's (2018) five practices for orchestrating productive discussions naturally outline how we can plan for routines. These practices remind us to anticipate, monitor, select, sequence, and connect.

1. *Anticipate What Students Might Do During the Routine*

   Anticipating what students might do helps you consider how you will respond intentionally rather than randomly. Considering student ideas and misconceptions can also help you think about other prompts you might pose through the routine in subsequent days. You can start anticipating simply by thinking about how you would find the solution to the prompt. Throughout this book, you will find routines with particular skills and concepts, many of which share some of the reasoning and solutions your students may offer.

2. *Monitor Student Discussions During the Routine*

   Monitor means that you listen to students as they work on a problem or discuss their thinking, particularly when discussing with a partner or small group. Granted, it is unlikely that you can listen to every student conversation, but you can be strategic about the discussions you monitor. You may monitor discussions of targeted concerns. You may monitor discussions of students who have shown inconsistent performance with a specific skill or concept. You may plan to monitor different groups on different days to balance whose conversations you listen to and focus on.

3. *Select Strategy and Reasoning to Promote During the Routine*

   As with discussions during your core lesson, you have to be careful not to randomly select students for discussion during routines. A random selection may compromise the discussion. Anticipating what students might do or think during the routine can help you think about the conversations or ideas that you want to listen for when monitoring. This coupled with considering the strategies, reasoning, or possible misconceptions that you want to highlight can help you select students for sharing during whole-group discussion of the routine.

4. *Sequence Ideas During the Routine*

   Strategies and ideas should be sequenced during discussion to advance student understanding. Sequencing may be most challenging during a routine. In fact, careful, deliberate sequencing of ideas during a routine may be impossible due to time constraints or inability to monitor every discussion in the short amount of time. You may be able to offset some of the sequencing challenge with questions. To do this, we can pose questions that help students make connections between strategies, reflect on efficiency, and make use of structure and patterns within prompts. Here are some sample questions:

   - How is ____'s strategy similar to ____'s?
   - How is ___'s strategy different than ___'s?
   - How does this idea connect to something we have discussed recently?
   - Will this approach always work?
   - If we think about efficiency, how do these strategies compare?
   - What patterns do you notice in the expressions?
   - How did you use patterns to help you find your solution?

5. *Connect Strategies and Concepts During the Routine*

Your questions during routines should help students connect solution paths or varied reasoning. They should help students see connections between concepts. They should also help students make connections between numbers, operations, and representations. You may even make decisions on the fly to extend student reasoning to new situations or problems through your questions. We offer questions for each routine in this book to support and guide you in facilitating discussion and connecting strategies, skills, or concepts.

PRACTICAL ADVICE FOR ROUTINES

Routines can be a component of your instruction that should require very little preparation. They should be both useful and practical. You should use them in ways that complement who you are as a teacher, what you value in mathematics, and what your students need. We note some important advice for working with routines below.

Modify, Modify, Modify

Routines work with any skill or concept. You can change the content to match your students' needs. Change it to meet a specific purpose. Modify how the routine functions. We present ideas about how a routine should unfold, but this is only a guide. Consistently monitor how students interact with the routine. Compare their work with the intent. Adjust or modify as needed.

Identify or Create the Content or Topics

Identifying or creating the content for the routines may be the most complicated aspect of routines. Topics should be those that students need to further develop or refine. We offer many examples and modifications throughout this book to ease that challenge. Yet there are other resources for creating examples. The prime resource is your students themselves. Having students create the number prompts may offer added benefit as it gives them an opportunity for thinking deeply about the identified concept. You can have students write or create routine situations as a homework assignment. You might also have students create routine situations as independent work once they have completed an in-class assignment. Keep in mind that students should work with a routine before creating prompts or problems for it. Also keep in mind that students can design quite creative, complicated, or unique situations.

Use Routines Formatively

Routines are a good way to formatively assess students. They can help you determine student perspectives and reasoning. They can help you monitor student proficiency with previously learned skills and concepts. They can help you determine specific types of numbers and operations that you might reteach or revisit through mini-lessons and other activities.

Be Committed and Creative

It's possible that the first few times you use a routine, you might find the activity to be clunky. This is natural. Try to give the routine some time before cutting ties with it. You can also reflect on how you can make it better or how you might modify the content or process to improve its effectiveness. Be mindful, too, that reasoning, communicating about reasoning, and working with mathematics mentally may be new to your students. Because of this, it may take some time for them to get comfortable with a routine. As noted, you can creatively adjust or modify the routine to best meet the needs of your students and your style of instruction.

JUMP-START ROUTINES AT-A-GLANCE

	ROUTINE	DESCRIPTION	PURPOSE
1	Missing Numbers	Students consider open problems where some of the numbers are missing.	Develop reasoning about skills and concepts by considering multiple possibilities when numbers are missing in a problem.
2	Order Me on the Number Line	Students use a number line (or double number line) representation to develop thinking and reasoning about numbers, variables, and relationships.	Determine viable options for numbers or variables on a number line, and examine the relationship between such.
3	More or Less?	Students compare expressions to a known value.	Reinforce computational fluency and reasoning by estimating and determining reasonable answers by comparing estimates to a given benchmark.
4	Two Wrongs and a Right	Students consider the accuracy of different solutions.	Develop reasoning about skills and concepts by considering multiple possibilities.
5	A or B	Students compare two different quantities and determine if they are equal, if one is larger than the other, or if inadequate information is provided to make the determination.	Reason quickly and accurately about the relative sizes of two quantities, engage in logical and numerical analysis, and perceive that, in some cases, not enough information is provided to make such a decision.

NOTES

PART 2

JUMP-START ROUTINES

VIDEO DEMONSTRATIONS:

Missing Numbers,
Example 1

Missing Numbers,
Example 2

Order Me on the Number Line,
Example 1

Order Me on the Number Line,
Example 2

Order Me on the Number Line,
Example 3

More or Less?
Example 1

More or Less?
Example 2

More or Less?
Example 3

Two Wrongs and a Right,
Example 1

Two Wrongs and a Right,
Example 2

Two Wrongs and a Right,
Example 3

A or B

online resources All videos can be viewed at resources.corwin.com/jumpstartroutines/highschool

ROUTINE 1

MISSING NUMBERS

When the numbers are missing from a problem, students must first think about the concept or idea of the situation and then begin the process of seeking the correct numbers to enter into the problem. It is well known that when numbers are presented in a problem, students often ignore the concept and work with only the numbers. This routine pushes students to start with the concept first.

> Fill in the blank by finding the largest and smallest integers that will make the quadratic factorable (produce real roots).
>
> $$x^2 + 2x + \square = 0$$

ABOUT THE ROUTINE

Missing Numbers is a routine that uses various high school concepts and representations to develop student thinking and reasoning about numbers, variable hopes, and relationships. In this routine, students consider open problems where some of the numbers are missing and they must enter the numbers to satisfy a given condition. This activity is distinctive because often students identify numbers in a problem first without thinking about the concept, idea, or theorem. The strength of this routine is that it gives the instructor insight into students' reasoning. Moreover, there is often more than one correct answer, so students can think about many different pathways. This routine is inspired by the work of Marcy Cook and the website http://www.openmiddle.com/.

The majority of these problems

- often have multiple ways of solving them as opposed to a problem where you are told to solve it using a specific method,
- involve optimization such that it is easy to get an answer but more challenging to get the best or optimal answer, and
- appear to be simple and procedural in nature but turn out to be more challenging and complex when you start to solve it.

WHY IT MATTERS

This routine helps students and highlights Mathematical Practice 3 (construct viable arguments and critique the reasoning of others) and Mathematical Practice 7 (look for and make use of structure). It also helps students

- consider the conceptual understanding first,
- look for and manipulate patterns and structure within relationships,

online resources All tasks can be downloaded for your use at resources.corwin.com/jumpstartroutines/highschool

- develop confidence with conceptual understanding and computation,
- communicate their reasoning with others, and
- listen actively to the reasoning of others.

WHAT THEY SHOULD UNDERSTAND FIRST

Students must first understand the conceptual underpinning of the example. The content of the examples draws from algebra, geometry, and algebra II. Sufficient content knowledge of the given is necessary for students to explore the problems.

WHAT TO DO

1. Draw or project the problem and the given constraints for the missing numbers.
2. Give students a few minutes to use various strategies (guess/check, graphing calculators, or known theorems) to solve for the missing numbers.
3. Students can be encouraged to use any tools they usually have access to (textbook, notes, calculators, computers, people, etc.).
4. Have students share their results with classmates in small groups or with partners.
5. Bring the class together. Ask students to share their responses.
6. After student ideas are collected, discuss the solutions offered by the class.
7. Honor and explore both accurate and flawed reasoning.
8. Explore additional values if time permits.

ANTICIPATED STRATEGIES FOR THIS EXAMPLE

In this example, many students will initially realize that when filling in the block with 1, the expression is factorable as $(x+1)^2$. And when $x>1$, the expression has no real roots. For all values of $x<1$, the expression will always have two real roots. This could also be seen by graphing the expression and using a slider for the value of the missing number. Moreover, students could examine the discriminant and determine when it is greater than or equal to zero.

> Fill in the blank by finding the largest and smallest integers that will make the quadratic factorable (produce real roots).
>
> $$x^2+2x+\square=0$$

ADDITIONAL EXAMPLES

ALGEBRA

This first group of examples (1–14) highlights problem solving and reasoning with algebra. In many of the examples, it is not necessary to actually solve for x but rather to reason or use number sense to determine the sign of the variable. If students use guess/check to find numbers that "work," you might ask students to find another solution or generalize the solution.

1 Insert any numbers between 1 and 9 only to make the equation have an integer solution > 0.

$\square x + \square = \square x + \square$

1. Answers will vary here, such as

$3x + 4 = 2x + 5$ and thus $x = 1$

Generally, if we have $ax + b = cx + d$ and want $x > 0$, then one possible way is to let $a > c$ and $b < d$.

2 Insert any numbers between 1 and 9 only to make the equation have NO solution.

$\square x + \square = \square x + \square$

2. To have no solution, both coefficients of x must be the same number and the other two blanks must be different numbers. Here is an example: $3x + 7 = 3x + 4$

3 Insert only the numbers between 1 and 4 to create an equation with a solution as close as possible to 0.

$\square x + \square = \square x + \square$

3. The 24 possible ways to do this are:

$x + 2 = 3x + 4$	$2x + 1 = 3x + 4$
$x + 2 = 4x + 3$	$2x + 1 = 4x + 3$
$x + 3 = 2x + 4$	$2x + 3 = x + 4$
$x + 3 = 4x + 2$	$2x + 3 = 4x + 1$
$x + 4 = 2x + 3$	$2x + 4 = x + 3$
$x + 4 = 3x + 2$	$2x + 4 = 3x + 1$
$3x + 1 = 2x + 4$	$4x + 1 = 2x + 3$
$3x + 1 = 4x + 2$	$4x + 1 = 3x + 2$
$3x + 2 = x + 4$	$4x + 2 = x + 3$
$3x + 2 = 4x + 1$	$4x + 2 = 3x + 1$
$3x + 4 = x + 2$	$4x + 3 = x + 2$
$3x + 4 = 2x + 1$	$4x + 3 = 2x + 1$

4 Insert numbers between 1 and 9 only to create an equation with a solution as close as possible to 0.

$\square x + \square = \square x + \square$

4. There are many equations that will get to the correct answer of 1/8 or –1/8. Here are some examples:

$9x + 3 = 1x + 4$
$1x + 7 = 9x + 8$

5 Enter any single-digit numbers between 0 and 9 (using each digit once only) in the boxes to create two linear equations so that the solution or intersection point is (1, 2).

$y = \square x + \square$

$y = \square x + \square$

5. There are many solutions here. Given the point (1, 2), students might quickly use $y = 2x$ as one equation. Another possible line would be $y = 5x - 3$

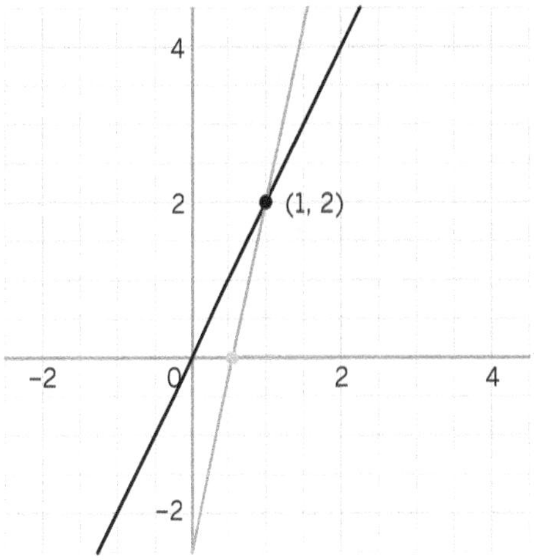

6 Enter numbers between 0 and 9 (using each digit once only) in the boxes to create two linear equations that are parallel.

$\square x + \square y = \square$

$\square x + \square y = \square$

6. For the two lines to be parallel, their slopes must be equal, but students cannot use the same numbers in the boxes, so creating a solution is trickier than it seems. Here is one example:

$x + 2y = 3$
$4x + 8y = 5$

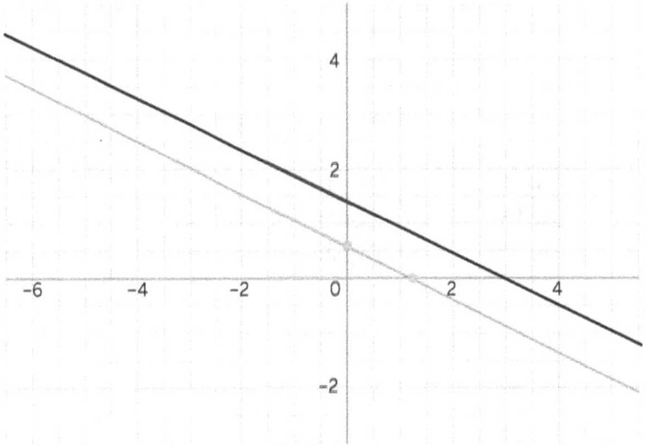

Follow up: What is the common characteristic of all students' answers?

7 Enter numbers in the boxes to create two linear equations that are perpendicular.

$\square x + \square y = \square$

$\square y = \square x + \square$

7. For the two lines to be perpendicular, their slopes must be negative reciprocals. Here is one possible answer:

$x + 2y = 3$
$4y = 8x + 5$

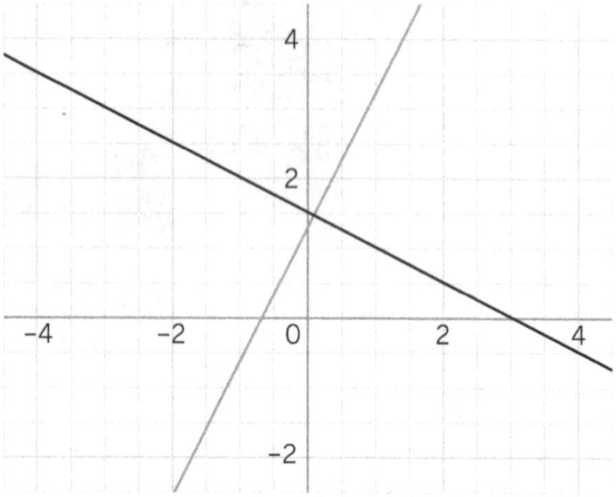

8 Fill in the boxes in the quadratic equation (with numbers between 1 and 9) such that the distance between the x-intercepts is 5.

$y = f(x) = \square x^2 + \square x - \square$

8. Think about this problem in factored form first $(x - a)(x - b) = 0$ and the distance between a and b is 5. Here is one possible solution:

$(x + 4)(x - 1) = x^2 + 3x - 4$

How many additional solutions can be found?

9 Fill in the boxes (with numbers between 1 and 9) in the quadratic equation such that the roots are whole numbers.

$\square x^2 - \square x + \square = 0$

9. Think about this problem in factored form first $(x - a)(x - b) = 0$

$(x - 4)(x - 1) = x^2 - 5x + 4$ is one possible solution as the roots are 4 and 1.

How many additional solutions can be found?

10 Fill in the boxes (with numbers between 1 and 9) in the quadratic equation such that there is only one real solution.

$\square x^2 - \square x + \square = 0$

10. Think about this problem in factored form first, $(x - a)(x - b) = 0$ and $a = b$ for only one real root to exist.

$(x - 1)(x - 1) = x^2 - 2x + 1$ is one possible solution as the root is only 1.

How many additional solutions can be found?

11 Using only the numbers 1, 2, 3, and 4 in each box below, create an equation such that $x = 1$.

$$\square x + \square - \square - \square x = 0$$

11. Here is one possible answer:

$2x + 3 - 4 - 1x = 0$

12 Create three linear inequalities using only the numbers 0 to 9 (cannot repeat a digit) that have (1, 2) in their solution set.

$$\square y < \square x$$

$$\square y < \square x$$

$$\square y < \square x$$

12. $y < 4x$, $2y < 5x$, and $3y < 7x$ is one possible set of inequalities that all have (1, 2) in their solution set.

13 Using only the numbers 1 to 9 as the coefficients of a quadratic function $0 = \square x^2 + \square x + \square$, what is the largest possible solution of the quadratic formula?

13. $a = 2$, $b = 9$, and $c = 1$

14 Fill in the boxes (ordered pairs) with numbers between 1 and 9 such that the slope of the line that passes through the points is as large as possible.

A $(\square, \square)$

B $(\square, \square)$

14. Largest slope is 8 using (2, 1) and (3, 9).

ALGEBRA VARIATION—NUMBER TILES

In examples 15 to 19, students use all the numbers 0 to 9 inclusive once and only once. It is helpful to have some tactile number tiles (just small pieces of papers about 1 in. × 1 in.) to move around the empty boxes to solve the problem. By doing so, students may persevere during the problem solving and not be frustrated by having to erase each time a number doesn't work in the empty box.

15 Using all the numbers 0 to 9 once, complete the following:

$x = \square$

$y = \square$

$3y^2 = \square\square$

$10(x + y) = \square\square$

$23y = \square\square$

$y^2 + 5 = \square\square$

15. Solution:

$x = \boxed{5}$

$y = \boxed{3}$

$3y^2 = \boxed{2}\boxed{7}$

$10(x + y) = \boxed{8}\boxed{0}$

$23y = \boxed{6}\boxed{9}$

$y^2 + 5 = \boxed{1}\boxed{4}$

16 If $x = 4$, use all the numbers 0 to 9 once to complete the following:

$2y^2 - 8 = \square\square$

$2y = \square 4$

$xy = \square\square$

$7 - y = \square$

$8y = \square\square$

$y - x + 1 = \square$

$y = \square$

16. Solution:

$2y^2 - 8 = \boxed{9}\boxed{0}$

$2y = \boxed{1}\,4$

$xy = \boxed{2}\boxed{8}$

$7 - y = \boxed{3}$

$8y = \boxed{5}\boxed{6}$

$y - x + 1 = \boxed{4}$

$y = \boxed{7}$

17 If $f(x) = 4x + 1$, then using all the numbers 0 to 9 once, complete the following:

x	$f(x)$
□	3□
12	□9
□□	81
□	2□
□□	7□

17. Solution:

x	$f(x)$
8	33
12	49
20	81
6	25
19	77

18 Using all the numbers 0 to 9 once, complete the following:

$x =$ □

$y =$ □

$y^2 =$ □□

$(x + y) =$ □□

$y - x + 3 =$ □

$24(x + y) =$ □□□

18. Solution:

$x = 8$

$y = 7$

$y^2 = 49$

$(x + y) = 15$

$y - x + 3 = 2$

$24(x + y) = 360$

19 If $f(x) = x^2 - 3x + 2$, then using all the numbers 0 to 9 once, complete the following:

x	$f(x)$
□	1□
1	□
□	20
□	□2
□□	96×95
□0	72
□	2

19. Solution:

x	$f(x)$
5	12
1	0
6	20
8	42
97	96×95
10	72
3	2

NUMBER AND QUANTITY

In this set of problems (20–24), students must use the digits 0 to 9 inclusive once and only once to answer the clues. It is recommended that the teacher orally read each clue once and allow students to use their number tiles to place the answer. When all the clues are completed, each digit from 0 to 9 will be used once.

20 Answers must use each digit 0 to 9 once and only once.	20. Answers:
Clue 1: Smallest integer value of an obtuse angle	91
Clue 2: Slope of the line passing through the points (1, 5) and (1, 10)	0
Clue 3: Slope of the line passing through the points (0, 5) and (3, 1)	5
Clue 4: Area of a circle with diameter 2 rounded to nearest integer	3
Clue 5: Area of a square with length = 8 and width = 6	48
Clue 6: $5^2 + 1$	26
Clue 7: The fourth prime number	7

21 Answers must use each digit 0 to 9 once and only once.	21. Answers:
Clue 1: Tenth and hundredth places of π	14
Clue 2: Number of sides of a heptagon.	7
Clue 3: Area of a triangle with base 12 and height 6	36
Clue 4: Hypotenuse length of a right triangle with legs 7 and 24	25
Clue 5: 2^3	8
Clue 6: Degrees in a right angle	90

22 Answers must use each digit 0 to 9 once and only once.	22. Answers:
Clue 1: Degrees in each part of a bisected straight angle	90
Clue 2: Only even prime	2
Clue 3: Prime number closest to 49	47
Clue 4: $\sqrt{36}$	6
Clue 5: Inches in half a yard	18
Clue 6: Factor of our largest single-digit number	3
Clue 7: Number of angles on a pentagon	5

23 Answers must use each digit 0 to 9 once and only once.	23. Answers:
Clue 1: 3!	6
Clue 2: $\sqrt{625}$	25
Clue 3: Number pointed to by the larger clock hand when the time is 15 minutes before an hour	9
Clue 4: Smallest two-digit number	10
Clue 5: Solution to $x - 2 = 81$	83
Clue 6: Degrees in an acute angle greater than 50	74

24 Answers must use each digit 0 to 9 once and only once.	24. Answers:
Clue 1: Product of 9 and 5	45
Clue 2: Number of sides on a hexagon	6
Clue 3: Largest single-digit prime number	7
Clue 4: Largest two-digit multiple of 15	90
Clue 5: Number of inches in a yard	18
Clue 6: Two more than a multiple of 7	32

GEOMETRY

In this set of examples (25–30), students might use graph paper, a graphing calculator, or the desmos app to explore multiple solutions on the coordinate plane. Examples 29 and 30 highlight triangle sum and volume of a cylinder.

25 Fill in the boxes (ordered pairs) with numbers between 1 and 9 to create a right triangle ABC.

A (☐,☐)

B (☐,☐)

C (☐,☐)

25. Multiple solutions are possible including these:

(1, 3)(2, 6)(8, 4)

(1, 7)(2, 8)(4, 6)

(1, 6)(3, 8)(4, 7)

26 Fill in the boxes (ordered pairs) with numbers between 1 and 9 to create a line segment with greater possible length.

A (☐,☐)

B (☐,☐)

26.

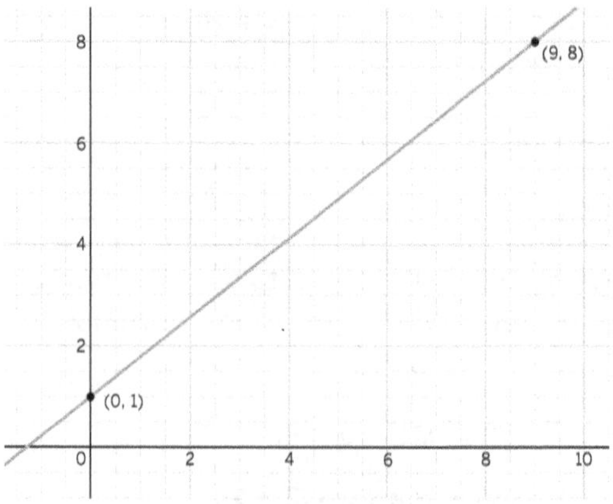

One possible solution is A (0, 1) and B (9, 8) with the distance of AB = 11.4.

NOTES

27 One vertex of a square is at (6, 0). Fill in the boxes (ordered pairs) with numbers between 1 and 9 to complete the square.

(☐,☐)

(☐,☐)

(☐,☐)

27. One possible solution is shown below.

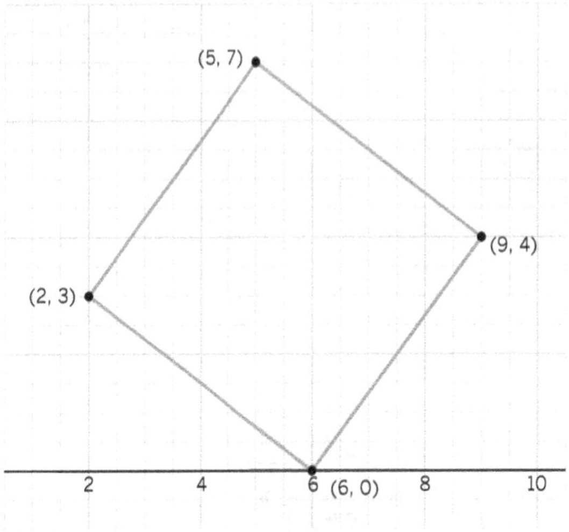

28 Fill in the blanks with the numbers 1 to 9 to create two points equidistant from (3, 4).

(☐,☐)

(☐,☐)

28. One possible solution is shown below. Both points are $\sqrt{8}$ away from (3, 4). This could also be seen by drawing slope triangles and displaying that each point is 2 away from (3, 4) in both the x and y distance.

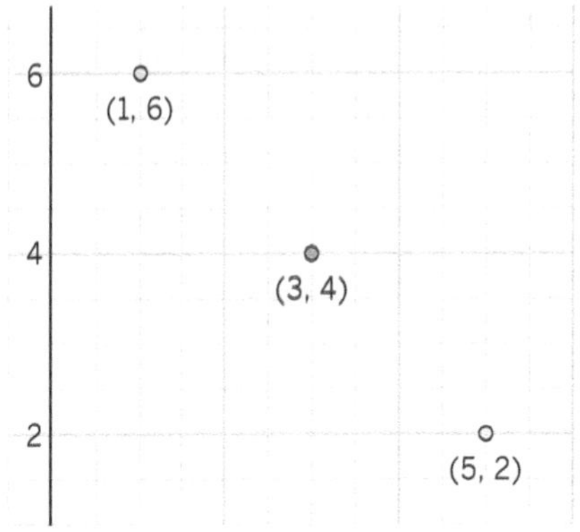

NOTES

29 Fill in the blanks with the numbers 1 to 9 (cannot repeat a digit) in the picture below.

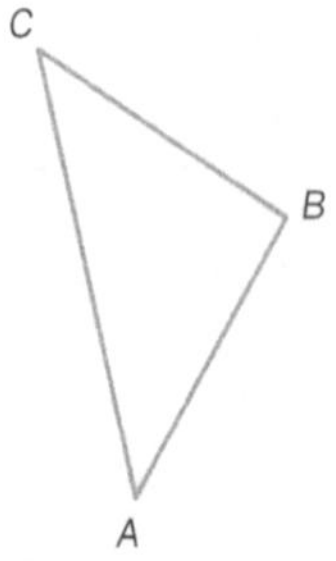

$\measuredangle A = \square\square^\circ$

$\measuredangle B = \square\square^\circ$

$\measuredangle C = \square\square^\circ$

29. The angles must add to 180; thus, one possible solution is 81, 64, and 35. Are there others? (Just move the unit digits around.)

30 A right cylinder holds between 110 and 115 cubic feet of water. Using whole numbers only, find three different values of the radius and height such that the volume is between 110 and 115 cubic feet.

$r_1 = \square$
$h_1 = \square$

$r_2 = \square$
$h_2 = \square$

$r_3 = \square$
$h_3 = \square$

30. Given the volume of a cylinder:

$110 < \pi r^2 h < 115$

Thus,

$35.01 < r^2 h < 36.6$

Thus, $r^2 h = 36$ would be a possible solution.

$r = 2, h = 9$

$r = 3, h = 4$

$r = 6, h = 1$

ROUTINE 2

ORDER ME ON THE NUMBER LINE

Order the following expressions on the number line:

n^2 | $\frac{n}{2}+1$ | $3n$ | $\frac{5}{n}$ | $\sqrt{n}$

(1) If $n = 1$

(2) If $n = 2$

ABOUT THE ROUTINE

Understanding how numbers and variables relate to one another is a hallmark of number sense. A refined understanding of number relationships is evident when we recognize that any one number has an infinite variety of relationships. This understanding enables us to think flexibly about numbers as well as derive efficient approaches to computation.

Order Me on the Number Line is a routine that uses a number line (or double number line) representation to develop student thinking and reasoning about numbers, variables, and relationships. In this routine, students consider the placement of numbers, variables, or expressions on a number line (or double number line). This activity is distinctive because, whereas often students just identify points on a number line, in this routine students are given a number line with a few initial values and then must order a list of values on the number line. With that information, students determine viable options for other numbers or variables and examine the relationship between such. As students share their ideas with classmates, they are exposed to different, justified possibilities. This discussion helps students develop more refined, flexible thinking about numbers and number relationships.

WHY IT MATTERS

This routine stresses Mathematical Practice 7 (look for and make use of structure) and Mathematical Practice 6 (attend to precision). It also helps students

- consider how a number relates to another number,
- reason about how two numbers relate to a third,

online resources All tasks can be downloaded for your use at resources.corwin.com/jumpstartroutines/highschool

- develop a sense of relative position and relationship (as the variable changes) on a number line,
- look for and manipulate patterns and structure within relationships,
- develop confidence with quantity and computation,
- communicate their reasoning with others, and
- listen actively to the reasoning of others.

WHAT THEY SHOULD UNDERSTAND FIRST

Students must first understand how number lines (and double number lines) work. They should be exposed to and comfortable with number lines. Students also need some foundational understanding of the values we use, including variables, expressions, and geometric vocabulary. Students might be challenged to think of numbers and their relationships in multiple ways. It is important to keep in mind that students do not need a flawless understanding of number lines or the numbers we incorporate into the routine. In general, these routines are intended to reinforce and enhance student thinking and reasoning about numbers, variables, relationships, and computation. For some students, these routines are opportunities for maintenance. But for many others, these routines will deepen their understanding of targeted skills and concepts.

WHAT TO DO

1. Draw or project a number line on the board (it may have given values depending on the example).
2. Give students the values that they will need to order on the number line. This could be done with index cards and thus students could move the cards around, engaging in a more tactile experience.
3. Have students share their results with classmates in small groups or with partners.
4. Bring the class together. Ask students to share their responses.
5. After student ideas are collected, discuss the solutions offered by the class.
6. Honor and explore both accurate and flawed reasoning.
7. Explore additional values if time permits.

NOTES

ANTICIPATED STRATEGIES FOR THIS EXAMPLE

In this example, students have five expressions to order with different initial values of n. When $n = 1$, students should quickly realize that n^2 and $\sqrt{n}$ are equivalent. Evaluating the remaining expressions (when $n = 1$) and plotting on the number line yields the following solution:

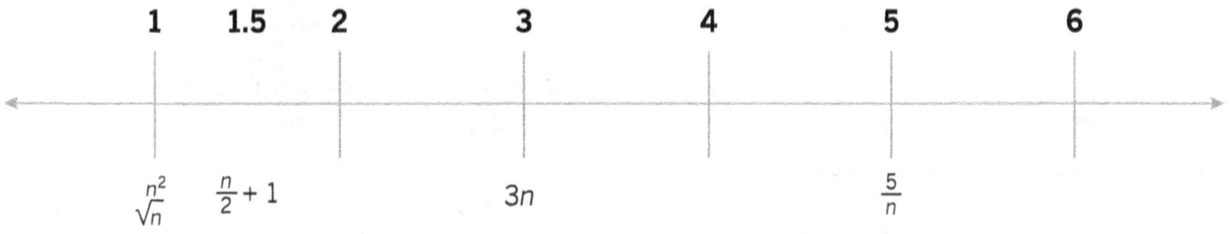

When $n = 2$, students need to reorder the expressions as follows:

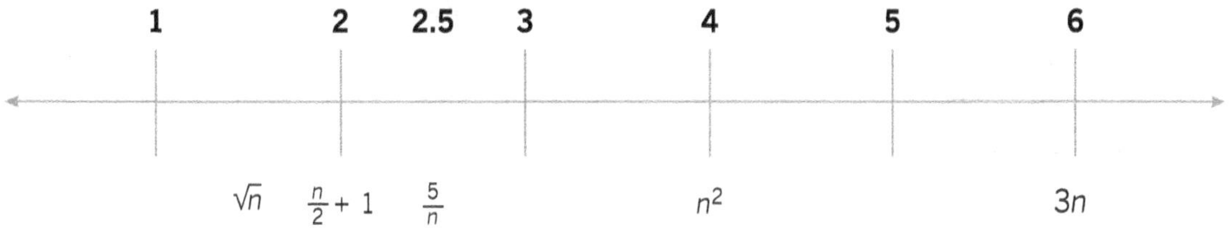

Students might also construct a vertical table (or number line), and you might ask several follow-up questions, such as these: What happens as n gets larger (which is subtly introducing the concept of limit)? Which expression is the largest when n is large?

NOTES

ADDITIONAL EXAMPLES

ALGEBRA

Single Number Line

In these examples (1 – 3), students must determine whether they can order algebraic expressions on a single number line. In some examples, a value is given for the variable, and in others, the variable in unknown.

1 Given $x^2 = 3x$ (and $x \neq 0$), plot x, $2x$, $3x$, $x+3$, x^2, and $\frac{1}{2}x$ on the number line.

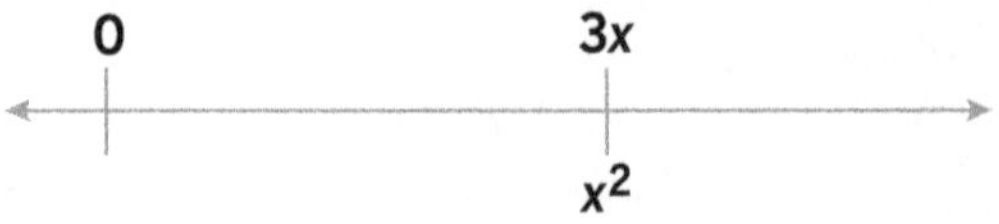

1. Since $x^2 = 3x$, we know that $x = 3$. Plotting the other expressions yields

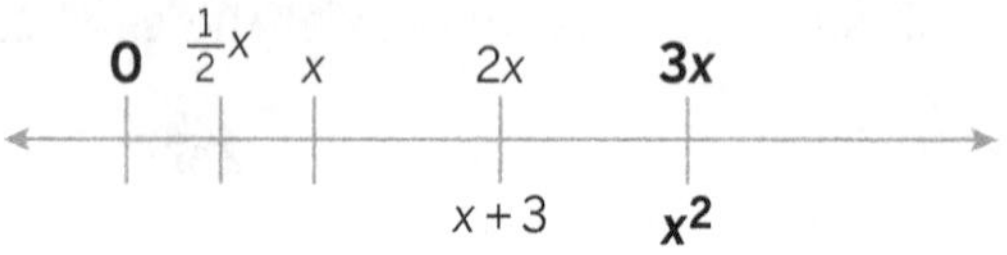

2 Given $b > a$ on the number line, plot $a + b$, $a - b$, $b - a$, and $\frac{a}{b}$.

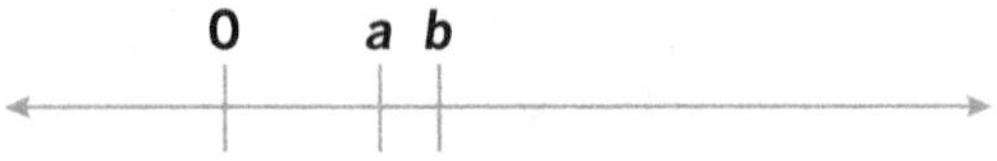

2. Students will attempt to plot $\frac{a}{b}$ in many places, but note that since we do not know where 1 is on the number line and the relationship of a and b to 1, it is not possible to plot $\frac{a}{b}$.

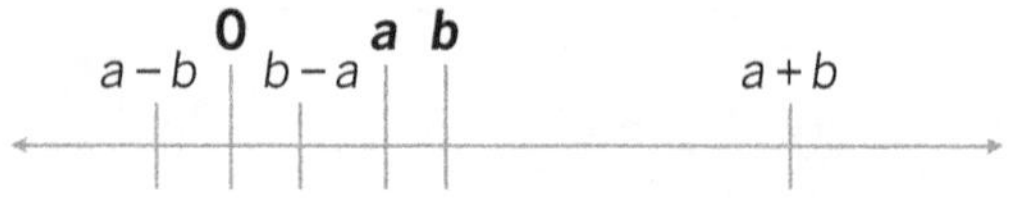

3 Given $-1 < a < 0$ and $b > 1$ on the number line, plot a^2, b^2, $\sqrt{a}$, and $\sqrt{b}$.

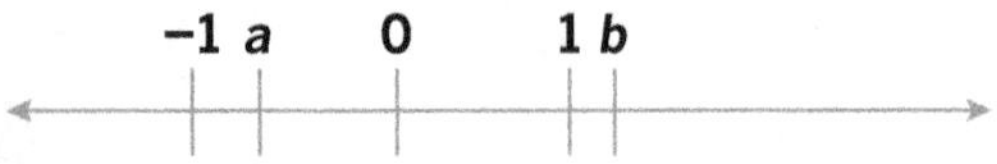

3. Note that $\sqrt{a}$ does not exist on the real number line.

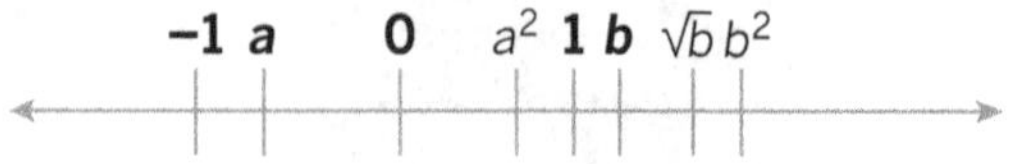

ALGEBRA VARIATION—WHO AM I?

In these variations (4–6), students are given several variable expressions on the number line and must determine a possible value (or values) for the given variable.

4 What is x?

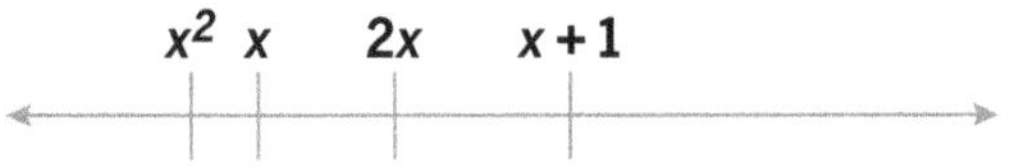

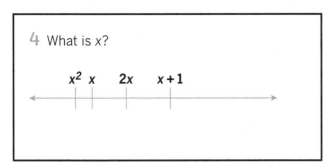

4. Since $x^2 < x$, $0 < x < 1$. A possible value for x would be $\frac{1}{2}$ and the number line would look like this:

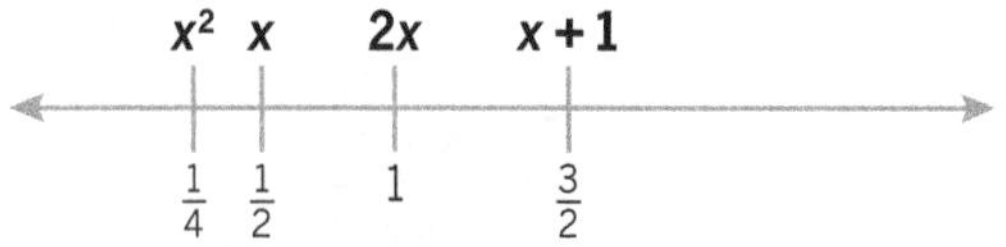

5 What is n?

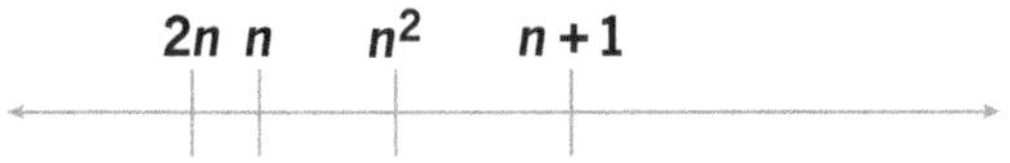

5. (a) If $2n < n$, then $n < 0$.

   (b) If $n^2 > n$, then $n < 0$ or $n > 1$ (ignore $n > 1$ due to (a)).

   (c) If $(n+1) > n^2$, then $(n^2 - n - 1) < 0$. Thus, $-0.618 < n < 1.618$ (this is the golden ratio). Due to (a) and (b) above, $-0.618 < n < 0$.

   One possible solution is $n = -0.5$, and the number line would look like this:

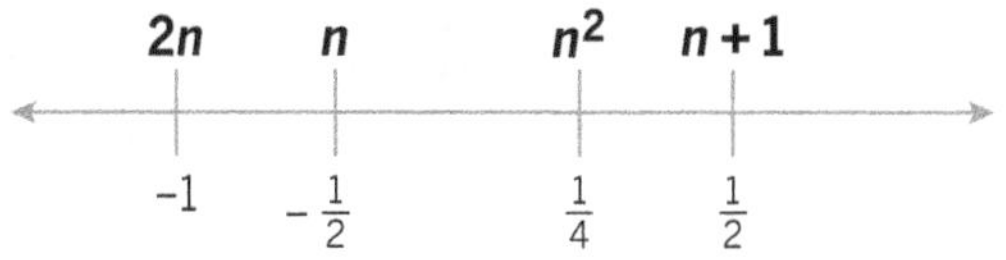

6 In this example, x, $3x$, and x^2 are arranged in three distinct orders on a number line. In each example, determine what x is equal to. In each example, x is a whole number.

A)

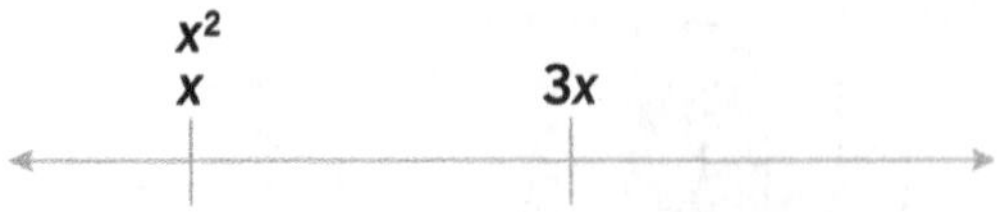

B)

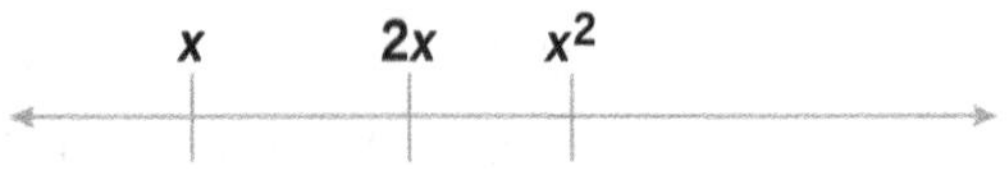

C)

6.

$x^2 = x$ yields $x = 1$ or $x = 0$, but since $3x \neq x$, then $x = 1$.

$x^2 > 3x$ yields $(x^2 - 3x) > 0$, which is true when $x < 0$ or $x > 3$. But since $x < 3x$, $x \neq$ less than 0. Thus, $x > 3$.

$x^2 < 3x$ yields $\left(x^2 - 3x\right) < 0$, which is true when $0 < x < 3$.

ALGEBRA VARIATION—DOUBLE NUMBER LINES

In these variations (7–10), two number lines are given with missing values on one or both. Students must plot equal values at the same place on the number line and fill in the missing values on each number line.

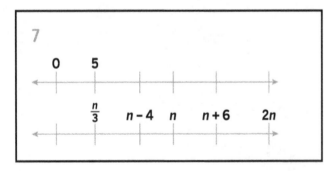

7

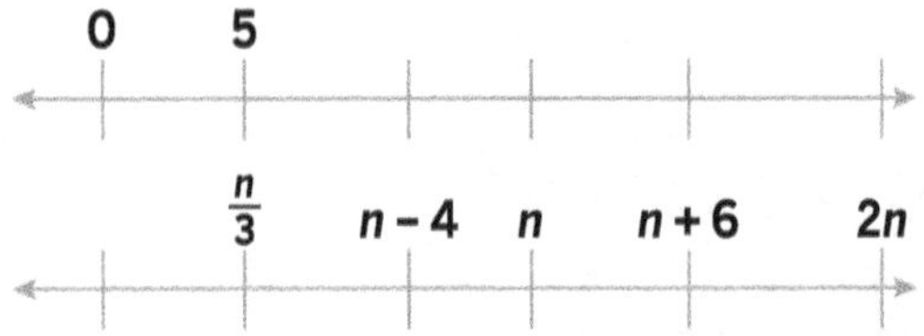

7. Since $5 = (\frac{n}{3})$, $n = 15$, which yields the following solution:

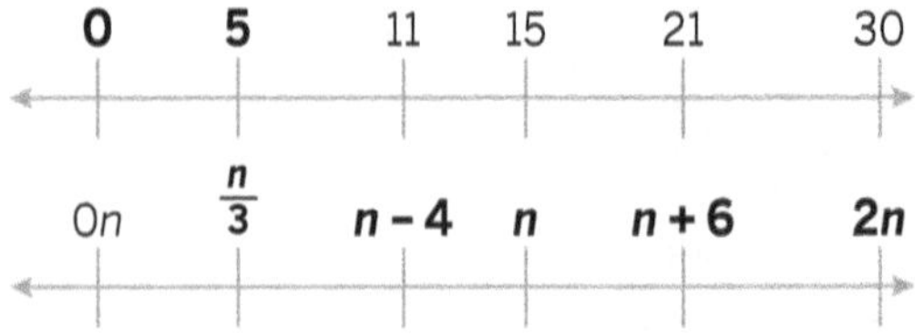

8

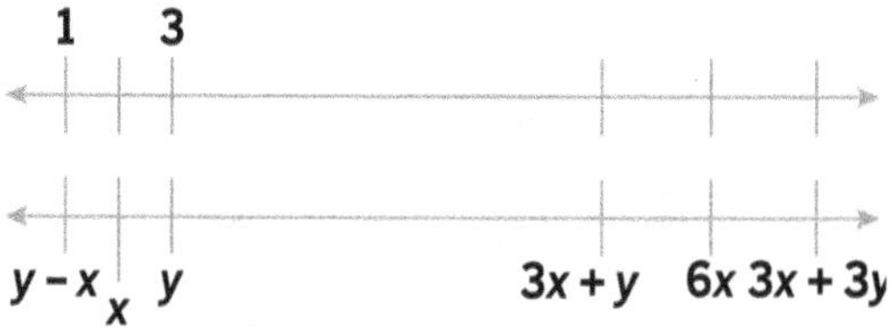

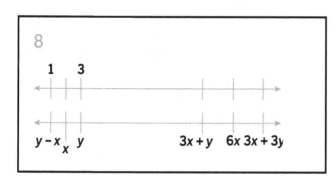

8. Given $y = 3$ and $y - x = 1$, $x = 2$ and the following solution is found:

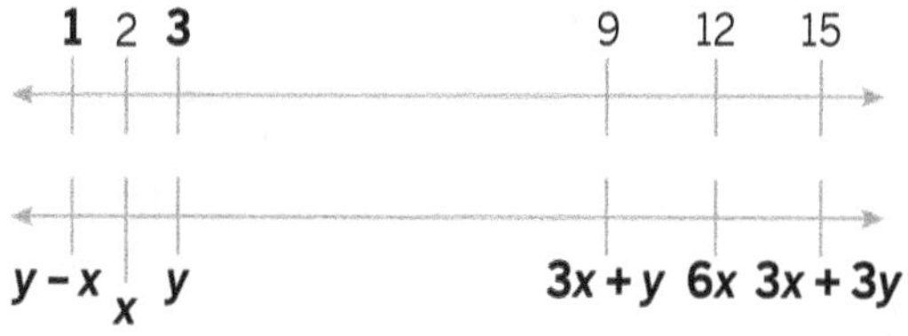

9 This example may lead students to question why $-5n$ is to the right of n.

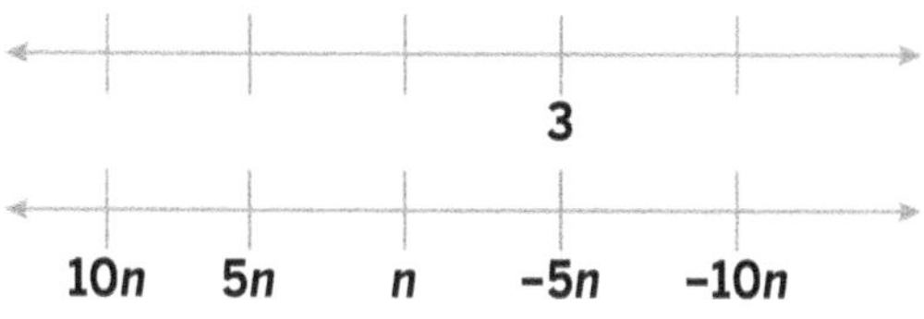

9. Since $3 = -5n$, $n = -\frac{3}{5}$ and the completed number line is as follows.

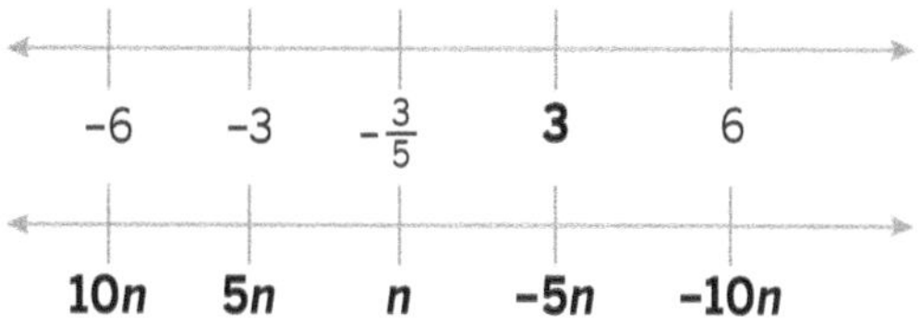

10 In this example, students do not see any values on the number line except the two given pieces of information. They must plot the missing values (numbers and expressions) on both number lines. In this case, plot x, y, x^2, y^2, and xy.

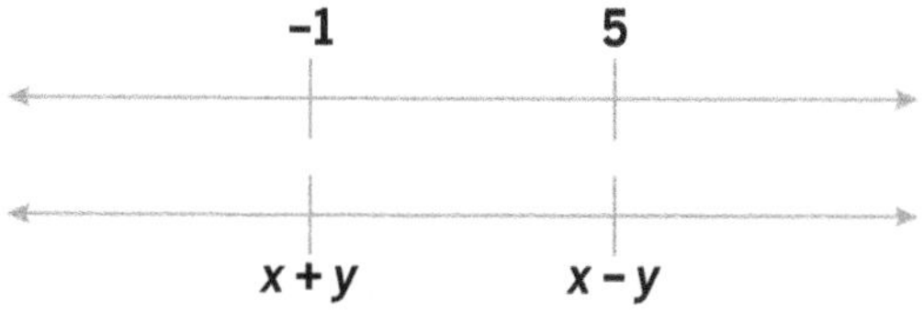

10. Since $x + y = -1$ and $x - y = 5$, by adding the two equations, $2x = 4$ and $x = 2$, substituting $x = 2$, we arrive at $y = -3$, and the solution number line is as follows.

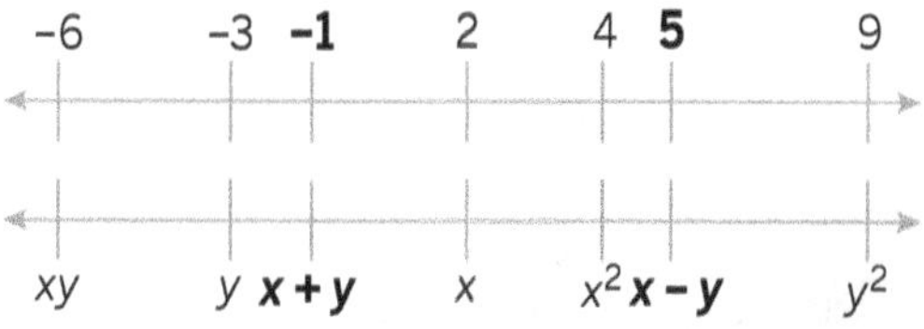

ALGEBRA VARIATION—GRAPHING

In these variations (11–13), students have to examine graphs of different functions and order various constants and parameters that are shown on the graph.

11 Given three lines with different slopes and y-intercepts, order m_1, m_2, m_3, b_1, b_2, and b_3 on a number line.

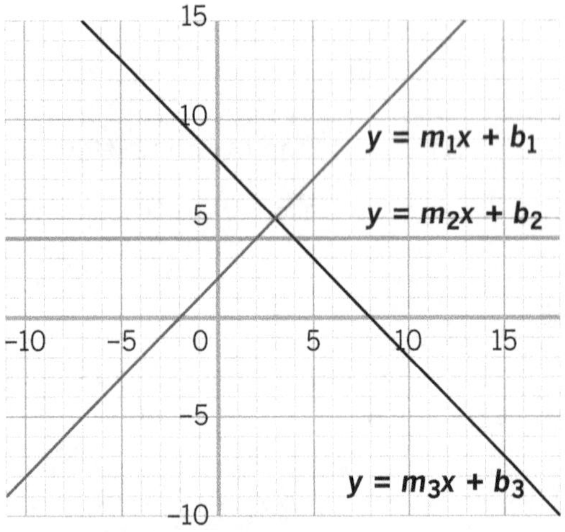

11.

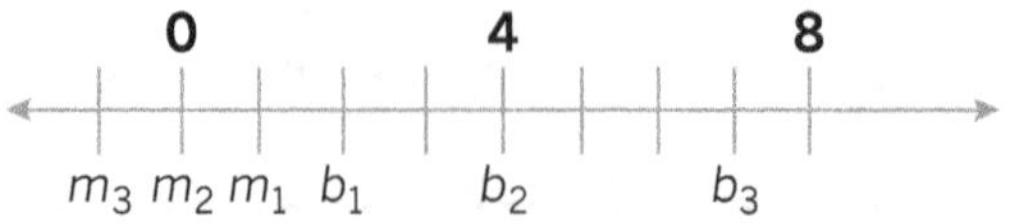

12 Given three parabolas with different a-values and k-values (y-coordinate of the vertex), order a_1, a_2, a_3, k_1, k_2, and k_3 on a number line.

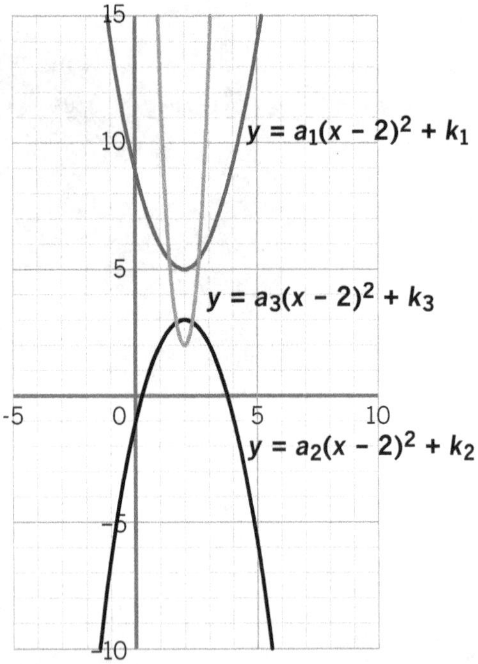

12.

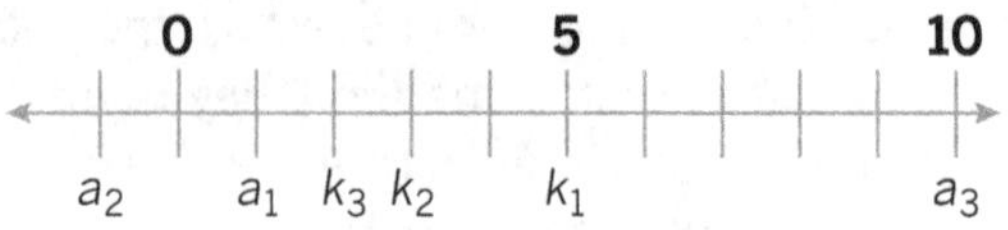

13 Given three exponential functions with different *a*-values and bases values, order a_1, a_2, a_3, b_1, b_2, and b_3 on a number line.

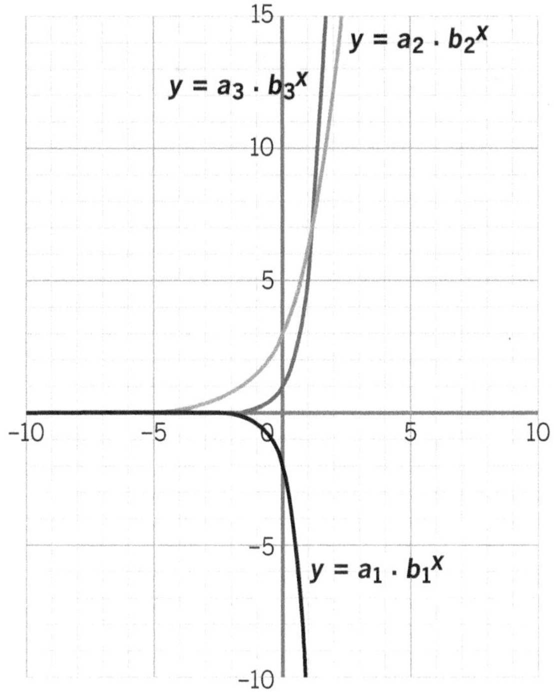

13.

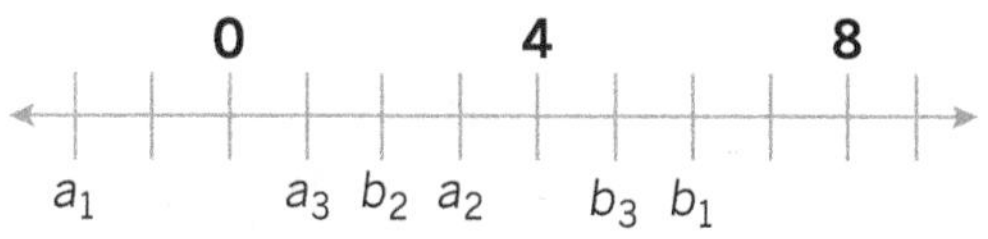

NOTES

GEOMETRY

In these versions (14–19), students have to examine different geometric properties and order variables that are shown on the figures. Note that it may not always be possible to find the exact value of each variable, but it is still possible to order them.

14 Given the two intersecting lines below, order a, b, x, y, $x+b$, and $b-a$ on a number line.

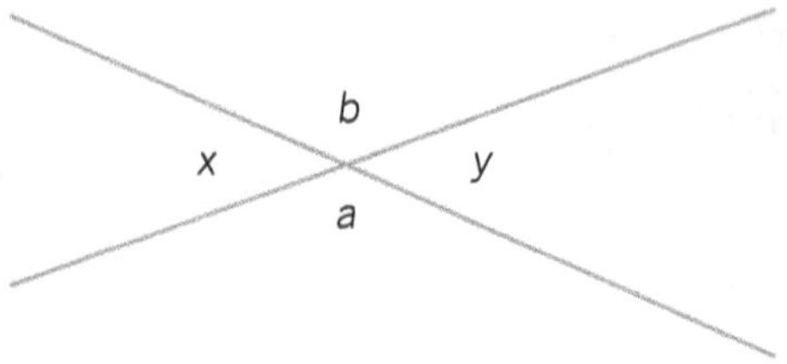

14.

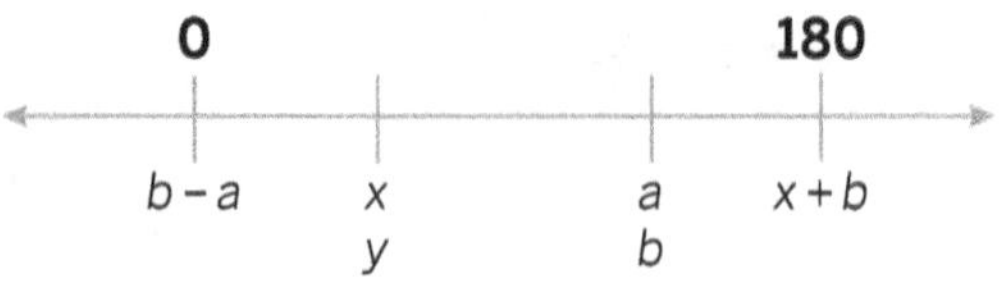

15 Given the two intersecting lines below, order a, x, y, and $2x+8$ on a number line.

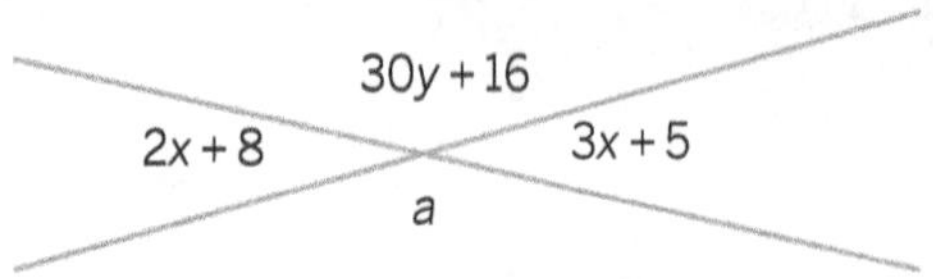

15.

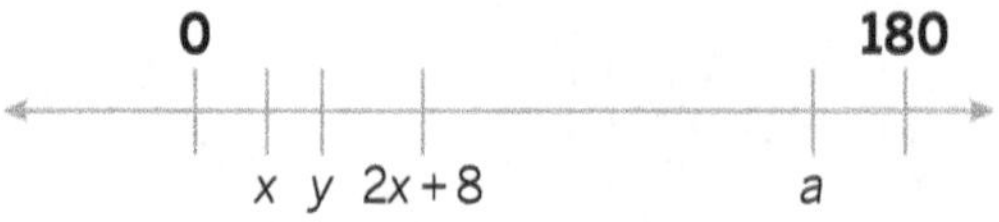

16 Given these two parallel lines intersected by a transversal, order a, c, $d-a$, $f+g$, and $b+c$ on a number line.

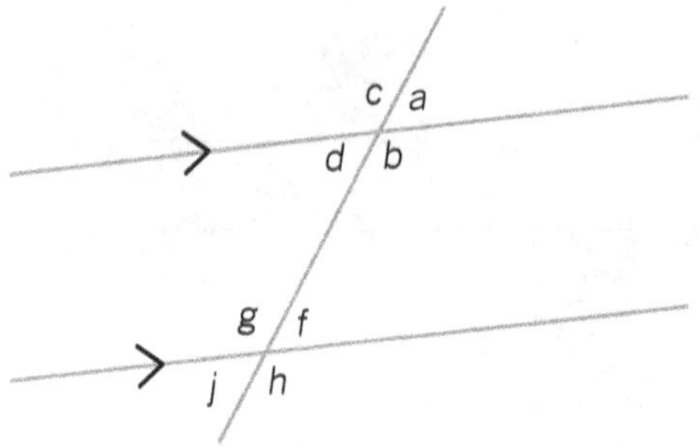

16.

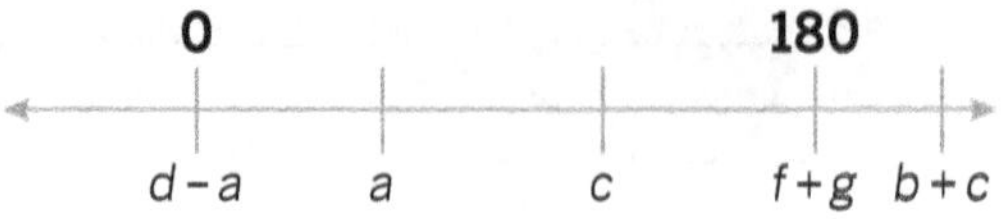

17 Given these two parallel lines intersected by a transversal, order a, $2a$, b, $2a+5$, and $2a+b+5$ on a number line.

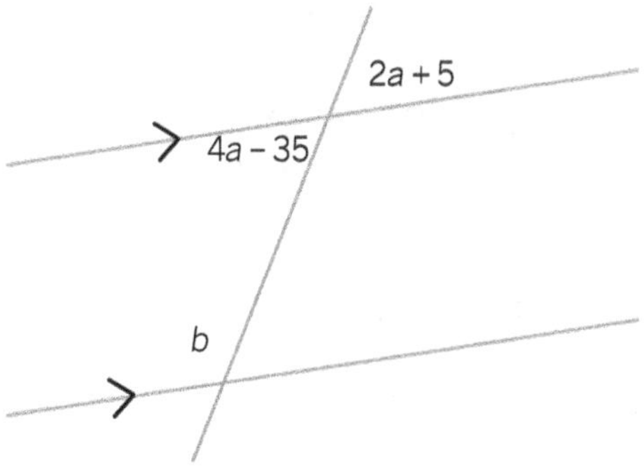

17.

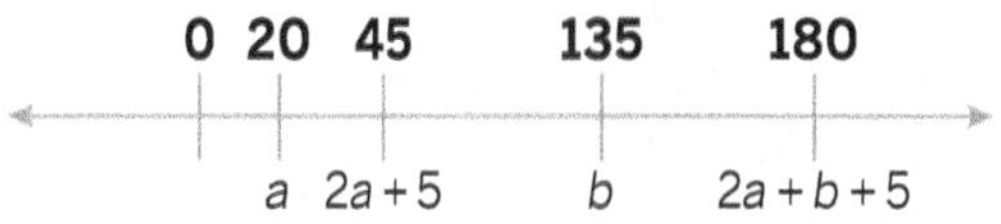

18 Given the isosceles triangle below, order a, b, c, and $a + b$ on a number line.

18.

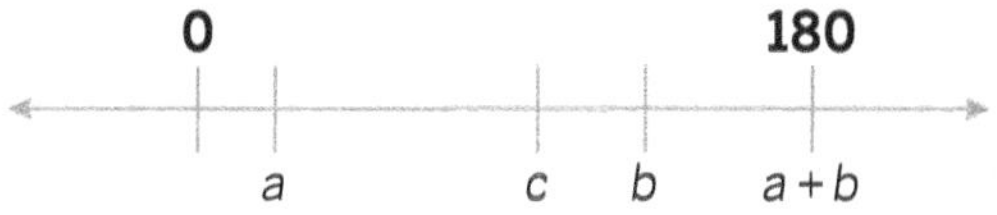

Some students might switch b and c on the number line or think that they cannot order b and c. But note that b is an exterior angle and thus equal to $c+a$.

19 Given the figure below, order a, b, c, d, and x on a number line.

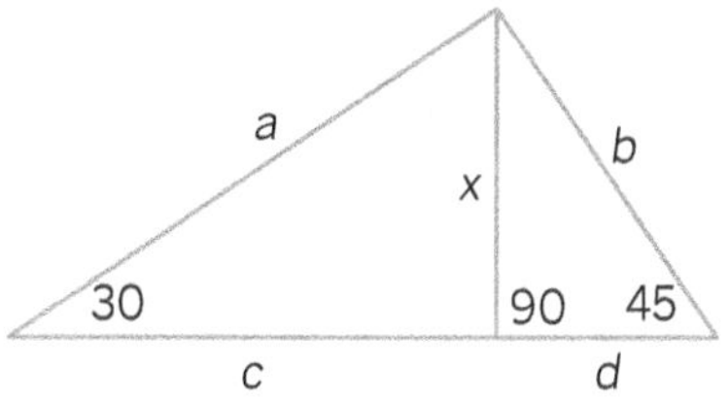

19.

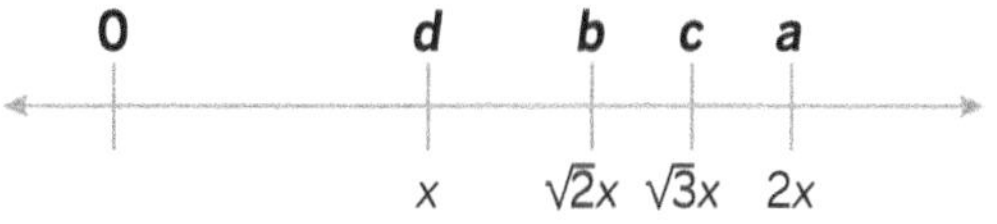

DATA ANALYSIS

In this set of examples (20–22), the data set is given and students must place statistical values on the number line. Challenge students to do so without calculating.

20 Given the data set below, place the median, mean, mode, Q1, and Q3 on a number line.

5	5	5	10	15	15	16

20.

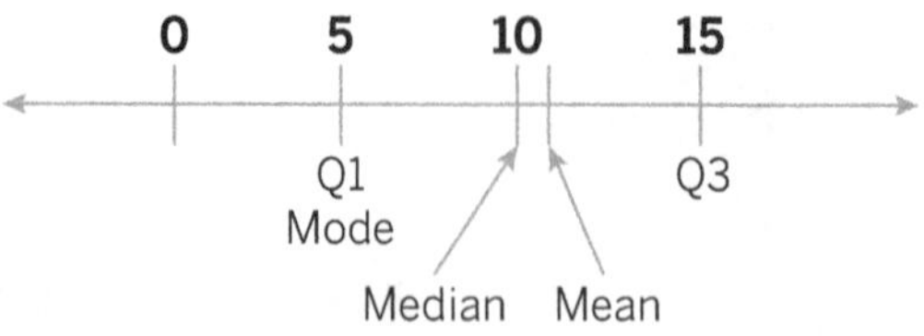

21 Given the data set below, place the median, mean, mode, Q1, and Q3 on a number line. Assume $x \geq 1$.

x	$2x$	$3x$	$4x$	$5x$	$9x$

21.

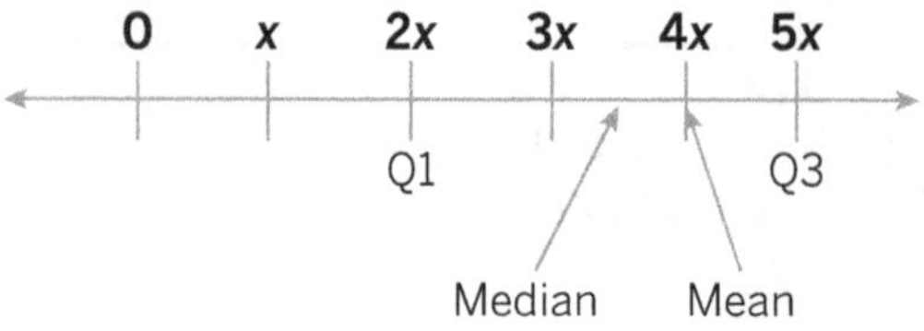

22 Given the data set $\{1, 2, 3, 4, \ldots, n\}$, place the median, mean, minimum, and maximum on a number line.

22.

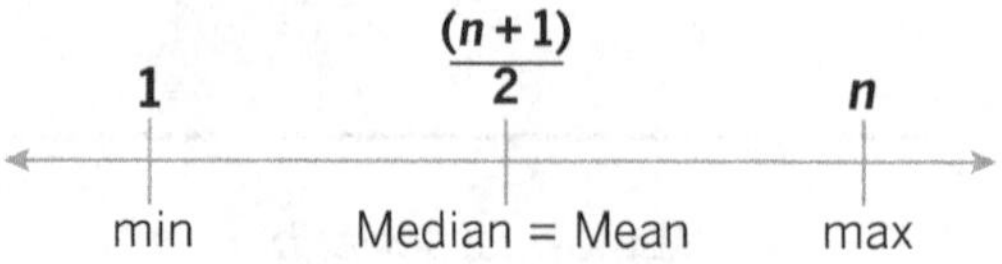

ROUTINE 3

MORE OR LESS?

ABOUT THE ROUTINE

"Is my answer reasonable?" We want our students to ask themselves this question every time they work with a problem or calculation. Yet many of our students don't often consider whether their answer is reasonable. They engage in mathematics mechanically. They blindly rely on procedures, pencils, or calculators to find solutions. Because of this, they may make computation errors or enter the wrong numbers on a calculator, having no idea that their result is impossible or wildly inaccurate. So is 2.7 + 1.7 more or less than 5? How do we know? How does knowing help us? These are the questions at the center of *More or Less?* In this routine, students make mental estimates. They compare their estimates to a given benchmark. They justify how they estimated the result and how it compares to the given value. This routine is intended to be a mental math activity.

Is the value of x more or less than 10?	
$x + 5.76 = 22.89$	$x - 5.76 = 22.89$
$x + 5.76 = 12.89$	$x - 5.76 = 12.89$

WHY IT MATTERS

This routine helps students with Mathematical Practice 2 (reason abstractly and quantitatively) and Mathematical Practice 7 (look for and make use of structure). In addition, it asks students to

1. determine efficient strategies for computing;
2. compare estimates with actual results;
3. estimate sums, differences, products, and quotients;
4. ask themselves if an answer is reasonable;
5. consider when and whether a calculation tool is needed;
6. identify whether their computations are accurate; and
7. defend their reasoning and the approaches of others.

WHAT THEY SHOULD UNDERSTAND FIRST

Before working with this routine, students should understand simple algebraic operations and geometric properties. They should have flexible computation strategies.

online resources All tasks can be downloaded for your use at resources.corwin.com/jumpstartroutines/highschool

WHAT TO DO

1. Present a few expressions, equations, or graphs to students.
2. Have them decide how the results will compare to a given benchmark. As noted, this is a mental mathematics opportunity. Students should not use tools to find exact values.
3. Provide time for students to reason.
4. Have students share their ideas with a partner before having a whole-class discussion.
5. Begin the whole-class discussion by identifying who believed which of the choices met the benchmark question.
6. Ask students to share how they made their decisions. As students share their thinking, it is important to probe thinking and ask clarifying questions rather than ask questions to establish how they thought about the expression. Here are some questions you might ask:
   - How did you estimate your solution?
   - Might there have been a more precise estimate?
   - Did you approach the expression in a different way?
   - How are different strategies similar?
7. Honor and explore both accurate and flawed reasoning.
8. Consider providing exact values after discussion so that students can compare and confirm their more or less estimates.

ANTICIPATED STRATEGIES FOR THIS EXAMPLE

Our students can and should reason about the value of a variable in equations. But they often go about solving equations by "doing to one side what is done to the other." And, as we know, the process can unravel quickly. But what if our students paused to consider whether an equation is simplistic enough to solve mentally? What if they were empowered to solve it without using paper and pencil? What if they reasoned about what the value of a variable might be before solving for it?

Students can approach each equation in various ways. Some students will consistently substitute the given value for the variable to make sense of what the true value might be. Some will consistently solve and compare the results. And some will guess and check possible solutions that they will then compare to the given value. There is nothing wrong with a preferred strategy. However, exposure to the strategies of others may help individuals refine their ideas about efficiency.

Is the value of *x* more or less than 10?	
$x + 5.76 = 22.89$	$x - 5.76 = 22.89$
$x + 5.76 = 12.89$	$x - 5.76 = 12.89$

In this example, strange unwieldy decimals are present in the equations to push students away from calculating toward mental mathematics.

- The top left (referred to as A) must be larger than 10 as 10 + 5.76 is not large enough to equal 22.89.
- The top right (referred to as B) must be larger than 10 as 10 – 5.76 is not large enough to equal 22.89. In fact, the answer to B is larger than the answer to A.
- The bottom left (referred to as C) is less than 10 as 10 + 5.76 would be greater than 12.89.
- The bottom right (referred to as D) is greater than 10 as 10 – 5.76 would be much smaller than 12.89.

ADDITIONAL EXAMPLES

ALGEBRA

In examples 1 to 19, the content is from the algebra curriculum. It is often the case that students do not have to actually calculate or compute the missing variable or information but can use algebraic reasoning and relationships to determine the solution to the example. Be mindful of this when listening to students' solutions.

1

Is the value of x greater or less than 0?	
$3.2x - 17.8 = 0$	$3.2x + 17.8 = 0$
$3.2x - 17.8 = 0$	$-3.2x - 17.8 = 0$

1. Students should not actually solve these equations, merely moving the constant term to the right-hand side of the equation and then examining the signs of the coefficient of x and the constant term. In the top-left equation, $3.2x = 17.8$, since both the coefficient of x and the constant term are positive, the solution will be positive.

   A) Top left: $x > 0$

   B) Top right: $x < 0$

   C) Bottom left: $x < 0$

   D) Bottom right: $x > 0$

2

Is the value of x greater or less than 1?	
$13.2x - 5.1 = 0$	$3.2x - 5.1 = 0$
$\frac{3}{4}x - \frac{12}{7} = 0$	$\frac{13}{4}x - \frac{12}{7} = 0$

2. Once again, students should not actually solve these equations, merely moving the constant term to the right-hand side of the equation and examining the fraction term that is created when dividing. In the top-left equation, $13.2x = 5.1$, and thus, $x = \frac{5.1}{13.2}$, which is less than 1. Students could also not see the need for dividing and the coefficient of $x >$ constant term.

   A) Top left: $x > 0$

   B) Top right: $x < 0$

   C) Bottom left: $x < 0$

   D) Bottom right: $x > 0$

3

Is the value of x greater or less than 0?	
$\frac{3}{4}x+\frac{12}{5}=10$	$-\frac{3}{4}x-\frac{12}{5}=10$
$\frac{3}{4}x-\frac{12}{5}=10$	$\frac{3}{4}x+\frac{51}{5}=10$

3. In the top-left equation, comparing the constants $(10-\frac{12}{5})$, we still have a positive number, and thus, dividing by $\frac{3}{4}$, a positive number, yields a positive solution for x.

A) Top left: $x>0$

B) Top right: $x<0$

C) Bottom left: $x>0$

D) Bottom right: $x<0$

4

Is the value of x greater or less than 1?	
$\frac{12}{7}x+\frac{3}{5}=3$	$\frac{20}{7}x-\frac{3}{5}=3$
$5x+\frac{13}{5}=3$	$\frac{1}{7}x-\frac{3}{5}=1$

4. In the top-right equation, comparing the constants $(3+\frac{3}{5})$, we have a number greater than 3, and thus, dividing by $\frac{20}{7}$ (a number less than 3) yields a solution greater than 1.

A) Top left: $x>1$

B) Top right: $x>1$

C) Bottom left: $x<1$

D) Bottom right: $x>1$

5

Does the equation have more or less than 1 negative root?	
$(x+4.8)(x+1.32)=0$	$(x+\pi)(x-1.8)=0$
$(3.7x+4)(3.9x+1)=0$	$(-2x-4)(-2x-1.92)=0$

5. In the top-left equation, students should notice that both expressions yield negative roots by examining the terms in the parentheses. $(x+4.8)=0$ yields $x=-4.8$. Is it even necessary to solve?

A) Top left: two negative roots

B) Top right: one negative root

C) Bottom left: two negative roots

D) Bottom right: two negative roots

6

Does the equation have more or less than 1 positive root?	
$(x-3.8)(3x+1.32)=0$	$(-x+\pi)(x-0.8)=0$
$(3x-4)(-3.9x+1)=0$	$(-3x-9.8)(-x-5.72)=0$

6. A) Top left: one positive root

B) Top right: two positive roots

C) Bottom left: two positive roots

D) Bottom right: zero positive roots

7

Is the graph's slope greater or less than 1?

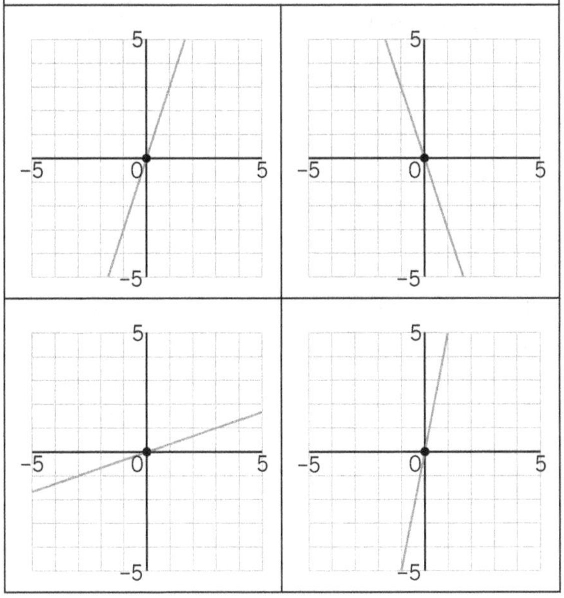

7. Students do not need to actually calculate the slopes of the lines but instead understand that $y = x$ has slope 1 and then determine if the line has slope greater than $y = x$.

A) Top left: slope > 1

B) Top right: slope < 1 (and in fact is negative)

C) Bottom left: slope < 1

D) Bottom right: slope > 1

8

Is the graph's slope greater or less than –1?

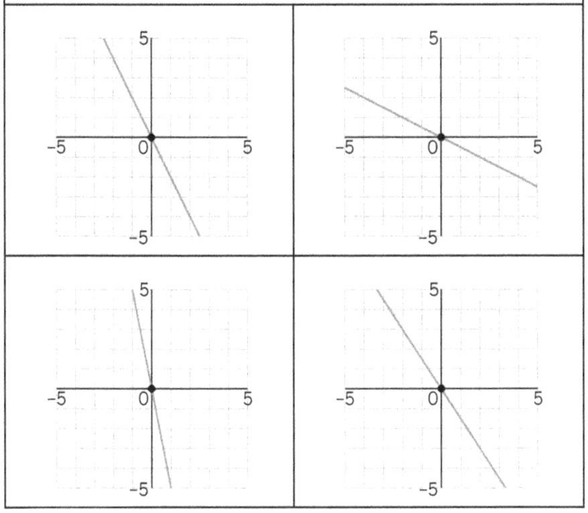

8. A) Top left: slope < -1

B) Top right: slope < -1

C) Bottom left: slope < -1

D) Bottom right: slope < -1

9

Does the line have a slope greater or less than 0?	
$\frac{3}{4}x+\frac{12}{5}y=10$	$\frac{3}{4}x-\frac{1}{5}=\frac{13}{5}y$
$\frac{3}{4}x-\frac{12}{5}y=10$	$-\frac{3}{4}x+\frac{12}{5}=\frac{-3}{5}y$

9. Once again, students do not need to actually calculate the slopes of the lines but instead examine the coefficients of x and y. The constant term has no effect on the slope.

A) Top left: slope < 0

B) Top right: slope > 0

C) Bottom left: slope > 0

D) Bottom right: slope > 0

10

Does the equation have a y-intercept greater or less than 0?	
$-\frac{1}{4}x+3y=-1$	$-\frac{1}{4}x-\frac{1}{4}y=-1$
$-\frac{1}{4}x+3y=-1$	$\frac{1}{4}x=3y$

10. To determine the sign of the y-intercept, students need to disregard the x-term and examine the sign of the y-term and the constant. In the top-left example $-3y=-1$, and thus, the y-intercept is positive.

A) Top left: y-intercept > 0

B) Top right: y-intercept > 0

C) Bottom left: y-intercept < 0

D) Bottom right: y-intercept = 0

NOTES

11

Does the line through the points listed in this table of values have a slope greater or less than 1?

x	y
1	5
2	7
3	9
4	11

x	y
1	5
1.2	7
1.4	9
1.6	11

x	y
1	5
4	7
7	9
11	11

x	y
1	5
3.1	7
5.2	9
7.3	11

11. To determine the slope (all examples are linear), students need to examine the change in the *y*-variables (always 2 in all examples) and divide by the change in the *x*-variable. For the top left example, we have $\frac{\Delta y}{\Delta x} = \frac{2}{1}$.

A) Top left: $\frac{\Delta y}{\Delta x} = \frac{2}{1} > 1$

B) Top right: $\frac{\Delta y}{\Delta x} = \frac{2}{0.2} > 1$

C) Bottom left: $\frac{\Delta y}{\Delta x} = \frac{2}{3} < 1$

D) Bottom right: $\frac{\Delta y}{\Delta x} = \frac{2}{2.1} < 1$

12

Does the line through the points listed in this table of values have a slope greater or less than 2?

x	y
1	10
2	15
3	20
4	25

x	y
1	10
3	15
5	20
7	25

x	y
1	10
4	15
7	20
11	25

x	y
1	10
3.6	15
7.2	20
10.8	25

12. A) Top left: $\frac{\Delta y}{\Delta x} = \frac{5}{1} > 2$

B) Top right: $\frac{\Delta y}{\Delta x} = \frac{5}{2} > 2$

C) Bottom left: $\frac{\Delta y}{\Delta x} = \frac{5}{3} < 2$

D) Bottom right: $\frac{\Delta y}{\Delta x} = \frac{5}{2.6} < 2$

13

Is the base of the exponential function greater or less than 2?

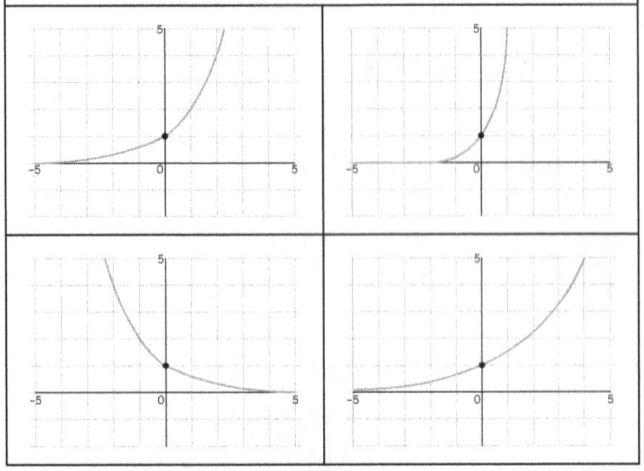

13. A) Top left: base = 2

B) Top right: base > 2

C) Bottom left: base < 2

D) Bottom right: base < 2

14

Is the decay rate of the exponential function greater or less than $\frac{1}{2}$?

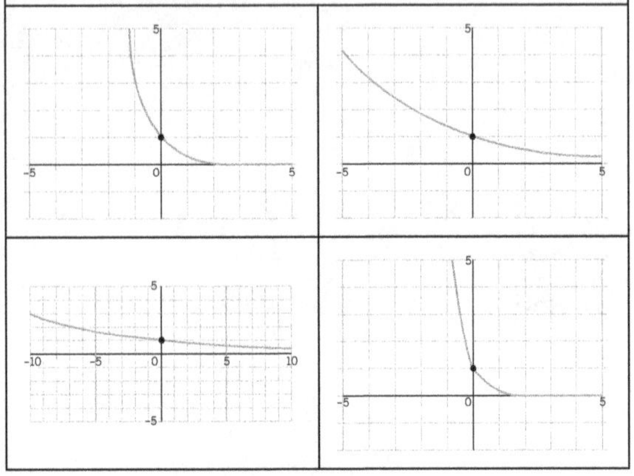

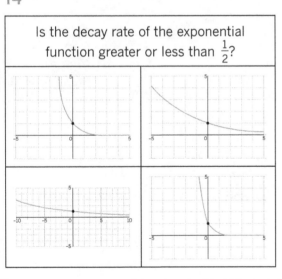

14. A) Top left: $\frac{1}{4}$

B) Top right: $\frac{3}{4}$

C) Bottom left: $\frac{9}{10}$

D) Bottom right: $\frac{1}{10}$

15

If $x > 1$, is the expression greater or less than 1?	
$\frac{x}{x+1}$	$\frac{-x}{1-x}$
$\frac{x+1}{x+2}$	$\frac{x}{x-1}$

15. This example asks students to compare the relative sizes of the numerator and denominator of each rational expression. Students might also graph the $y =$ (expression given) with domain $\{x > 1\}$

A) Top left: expression < 1

B) Top right: expression > 1

C) Bottom left: expression < 1

D) Bottom right: expression > 1

16

If $x < -1$, is the expression greater or less than 1?	
$\frac{x}{x+1}$	$\frac{-x}{1-x}$
$\frac{x+1}{x-1}$	$\frac{1}{x-1}$

16. A) Top left: $\frac{x}{x+1} > 1$

B) Top right: $\frac{-x}{1-x} < 1$

C) Bottom left: $\frac{x+1}{x-1} < 1$

D) Bottom right: $\frac{1}{x-1} < 1$

17

If $0 < n < 1$, is the expression greater or less than 1?	
$\sqrt{n}$	$\frac{1}{n}$
n^2	$n-2$

17. A) Top left: less than 1

B) Top right: greater than 1

C) Bottom left: less than 1

D) Bottom right: less than 1

18

If $0 < a < b < 1$, then is the expression greater or less than 1?	
ab	$\frac{a}{b}$
$\frac{b}{a}$	$a - b$

19

Is the unknown value more than or less than 36?	
When Austin is 12 years older, he will be 36. How old is he now?	After Jordyn reads 36 pages of her magazine, she still has 12 pages to read. How many pages are in the magazine?
When a package of candy is shared among 12 friends, each gets 36 pieces. How many pieces of candy were in the package?	Dakota's dog weighs 12 pounds more than Eric's dog. The dogs weigh 36 pounds together. How much does Eric's dog weigh?

18. A) Top left: $ab < 1$ (as both a and b are less than 1)

B) Top right: $\frac{a}{b} < 1$ (if $a < b$, then $\frac{a}{b} < 1$)

C) Bottom left: $\frac{b}{a} > 1$ (if $a < b$, then $\frac{b}{a} > 1$)

D) Bottom right: $(a-b) < 1$ and in fact $(a-b) < 0$ as $a < b$

19. A) Top left: unknown is less than 36 $(x + 12 = 36)$

B) Top right: unknown is more than 36$(x - 36 = 12)$

C) Bottom left: unknown is more than 36$\left(\frac{x}{12} = 36\right)$

D) Bottom right: unknown is less than 36$(x + x + 12 = 36)$

GEOMETRY

The next set of examples (20–27) reviews some basic areas of geometry including area, perimeter, volume, parallel lines, and right angle trigonometry. You might decide to provide the necessary formulas for your students when they are solving the examples.

20

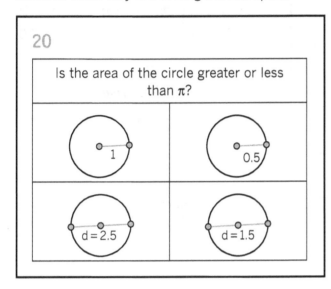

Is the area of the circle greater or less than π?

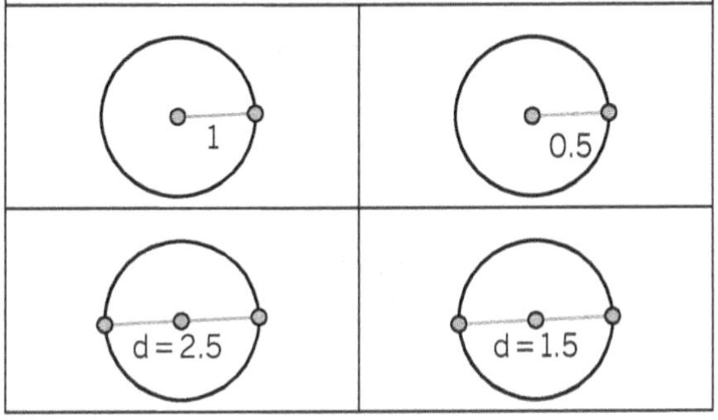

20. Since the area of a circle is πr^2, to see if the area > π, students need to determine only whether the radius^2 > 1.

A) Top left: radius$^2 = 1$, area $= \pi$

B) Top right: radius$^2 < 1$, area $< \pi$

C) Bottom left: radius$^2 > 1$, area $> \pi$

D) Bottom right: radius$^2 < 1$, area $< \pi$

21

Is the volume of the cylinder greater or less than 100π?	
Cylinder with base area = 25 and height = 10	Cylinder with radius = 3 and height = 5
Cylinder with diameter = 2 and height = 50	Cylinder with radius = 5 and height = 10

21. Since the volume of a circle is $\pi r^2 h$, to see if the volume > 100π, students need to determine only whether $r^2h > 100\pi$. But how does this change if the base area is given and not the radius?

A) Top left: base area × height = $250 < 100\pi$

B) Top right: $r^2h < 100$, thus $V < 100\pi$

C) Bottom left: $r^2h < 100$, thus $V < 100\pi$

D) Bottom right: $r^2h < 100$, thus $V < 100\pi$

22

Is the volume of the solid greater or less than 99?	
Cone with base area = 30 and height = 10	Cylinder with base area = 10 and height = 10
Cone with base area = 60 and height = 5	Cylinder with base area = 5 and height = 20

22. Since the volume of a cone is $\frac{1}{3}$ base area × height and the volume of a cylinder is base area × height, students need to compare these to a volume = 99.

A) Top left: $\frac{1}{3}$ base area × height = 100

B) Top right: base area × height = 100

C) Bottom left: $\frac{1}{3}$ base area × height = 100

D) Bottom right: base area × height = 100

23

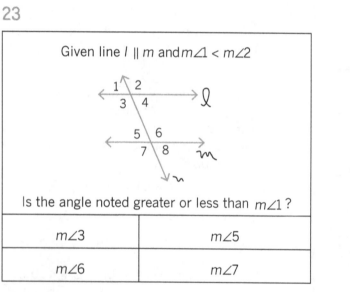

Given line $l \parallel m$ and $m\angle 1 < m\angle 2$

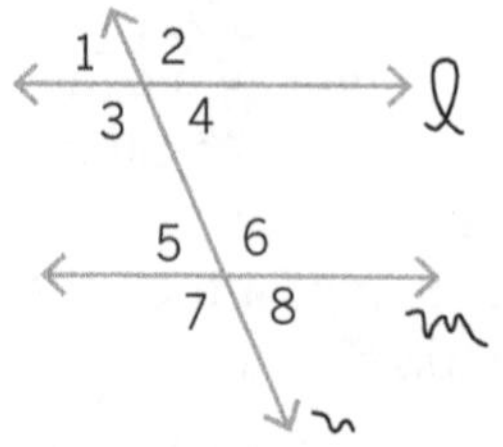

Is the angle noted greater or less than $m\angle 1$?	
$m\angle 3$	$m\angle 5$
$m\angle 6$	$m\angle 7$

23. To determine if each area is greater than or less than $m\angle 1$, students need to be aware of the relationships formed when two parallel lines are intersected by a transversal.

A) Top left: $m\angle 3 > m\angle 1$

B) Top right: $m\angle 5 = m\angle 1$

C) Bottom left: $m\angle 6 > m\angle 1$

D) Bottom right: $m\angle 7 > m\angle 1$

24

Is the ratio greater than $\frac{1}{2}$?

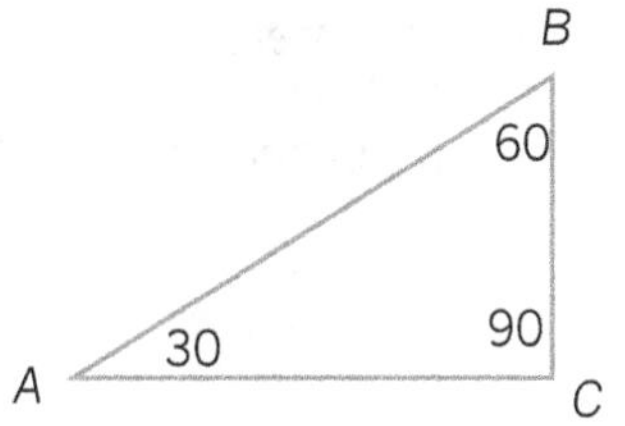

$\sin 30°$	$\cos 30°$
$\tan 30°$	$\tan 60°$

25

Is the hypotenuse greater or less than 5?

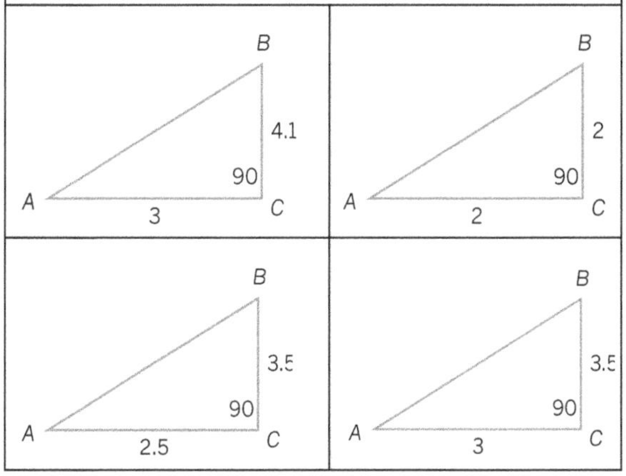

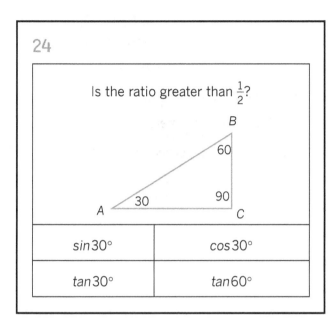

24. Students need to know their 30-60-90 triangle relationships in this example. The sides opposite the 30-60-90 angles are in a 1-$\sqrt{3}$-2 ratio.

A) Top left: equals $\frac{1}{2}$

B) Top right: greater than $\frac{1}{2}$

C) Bottom left: greater than $\frac{1}{2}$

D) Bottom right: greater than $\frac{1}{2}$

25. Students should recognize the Pythagorean triplet 3-4-5 and use it to make estimates about the hypotenuse of each figure.

A) Top left: greater than 5

B) Top right: less than 5

C) Bottom left: less than 5

D) Bottom right: less than 5

26

The area of each shape below is 5 square units. Is the perimeter greater or less than 11 units?

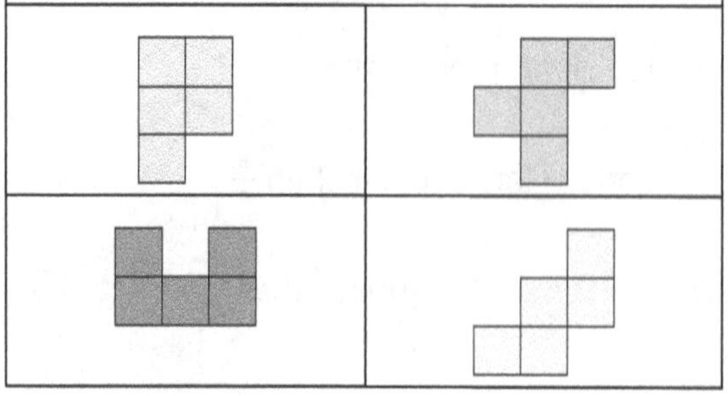

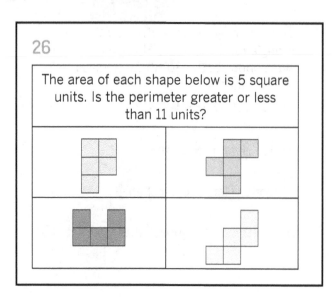

26. Although the area of each shape is the same, the perimeters are not constant.

A) Top left: perimeter $= 10 < 11$

B) Top right: perimeter $= 12 > 11$

C) Bottom left: perimeter $= 12 > 11$

D) Bottom right: perimeter $= 12 > 11$

27

Figure DECF is a rectangle. Is the shaded area greater or less than 20?

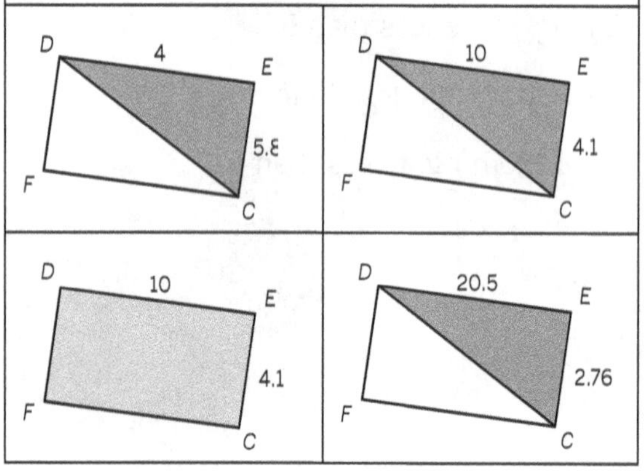

27. Students should recall area formulas for triangles and rectangles.

A) Top left: area < 20

B) Top right: area > 20

C) Bottom left: area > 20

D) Bottom right: area > 20

DATA ANALYSIS

The last three examples (28–30) involve basic probability and data analysis.

28

When rolling a single die, is the probability of the event greater or less than $\frac{1}{2}$?	
Prime number	Number > 4
Number with more than 2 factors	Odd number > 1

28. Students should quickly note that the sample space = {1, 2, 3, 4, 5, 6}.

    A) Top left: {2, 3, 5}, probability $= \frac{1}{2}$

    B) Top right: {5, 6}, probability $< \frac{1}{2}$

    C) Bottom left: {4, 6}, probability $< \frac{1}{2}$

    D) Bottom right: {3, 5}, probability $< \frac{1}{2}$

29

Is the mean of the given set of numbers greater or less than 10?	
{11, 11, 11, 9, 9}	{11, 11, 9, 9, 9}
{11, 11, 10, 9, 8}	{11.2, 11.1, 10, 9.8, 9.7}

29. There is no need to actually compute the mean of the data sets here. Students should use mental mathematics to think about how far the data points are from 10 in either direction.

    A) Top left: mean > 10

    B) Top right: mean < 10

    C) Bottom left: mean < 10 (compare it to the top left data set)

    D) Bottom right: mean > 10

30

The mean of each data set below is 10. Is the median greater or less than the mean?	
{3, 8, 11, 11, 17}	{–37, 5, 11, 14, 57}
{9, 8, 13, 13, 7}	{33, 38, 9, –51, 21}

30. Students might want to quickly confirm that the mean of each set is 10 (or note that the sum of each set is 50).

    A) Top left: median = 11 > mean

    B) Top right: median = 11 > mean

    C) Bottom left: median = 9 < mean

    D) Bottom right: median = 21 > mean

NOTES

ROUTINE 4

TWO WRONGS AND A RIGHT

Write the equation of a line in point-slope form that passes through (2, 5) and (5, 11). $m = \frac{11-5}{5-2} = \frac{6}{3} = 2$ $y - 5 = 2(x - 2)$	Write the equation of a line in point-slope form that passes through (2, 5) and (5, 11). $m = \frac{5-11}{5-2} = \frac{-6}{3} = -2$ $y - 11 = -2(x - 2)$
Write the equation of a line in point-slope form that passes through (2, 5) and (5, 11). $m = \frac{5-11}{5-2} = \frac{-6}{3} = 2$ $y - 5 = -2(x - 2)$	Two **wrongs** and a **right**

ABOUT THE ROUTINE

In *Two Wrongs and a Right*, students analyze the work of three mathematical arguments of which two are wrong and one is correct. Students determine which argument is correct and detect the mathematical errors in the others.

This daily routine has the potential to add considerable value to any classroom, as it provides students with repeated opportunities to develop their sense-making and argument-constructing/critiquing abilities.

WHY IT MATTERS

Why is it a good idea to have students analyze math errors?

- It promotes the use of several mathematical practices including Mathematical Practice 1 (make sense of problems and persevere in solving them), Mathematical Practice 2 (reason abstractly and quantitatively), and especially Mathematical Practice 3 (construct viable arguments and critique the reasoning of others).

online resources All tasks can be downloaded for your use at resources.corwin.com/jumpstartroutines/highschool

- It promotes higher level thinking. Error analysis is at the top of the higher level thinking skills hierarchy. It requires students to create, analyze, and even prove what is correct.
- It aids in conceptual understanding. When students can find errors in a process and explain it (that part is key), they are really showing a conceptual understanding of the skill or concept.
- It is a great test-taking strategy. Teaching students to find errors in thinking and algorithms is a perfect way to prepare them for multiple-choice math questions in an authentic manner. When they solve a math problem and are unable to locate the answer in the choice, they can look over their work and see if they can determine the error in their own math.

WHAT THEY SHOULD UNDERSTAND FIRST

Clearly, students should learn to identify their own mathematical errors and self-correct their mistakes. This routine gives students such practice and the ability to study mathematical errors to identify the cause of the incorrect answer. This ability to check for correctness is a big key to achieving math proficiency.

WHAT TO DO

1. Display the three mathematical arguments to the problem to the class.
2. Have students work in pairs to determine which of the three is correct and determine the error in the other two.
3. Facilitate student reflection and discussion.
4. Help students think about the *assumptions* behind each mistake, whether there are *fragments of correctness* in a given mistake, and how they might *help a classmate* who was prone to such a mistake.

ANTICIPATED STRATEGIES FOR THIS EXAMPLE

Students will likely analyze each step of the arguments presented as follows:

- Top left: The student calculated the slope correctly and used the point-slope formula correctly.
- Top right: The student calculated the slope incorrectly and used numbers from two different points in the point-slope formula.
- Bottom left: The student calculated the slope incorrectly.

Write the equation of a line in point-slope form that passes through (2, 5) and (5, 11). $m = \frac{11-5}{5-2} = \frac{6}{3} = 2$ $y - 5 = 2(x - 2)$	Write the equation of a line in point-slope form that passes through (2, 5) and (5, 11). $m = \frac{5-11}{5-2} = \frac{-6}{3} = -2$ $y - 11 = -2(x - 2)$
Write the equation of a line in point-slope form that passes through (2, 5) and (5, 11). $m = \frac{5-11}{5-2} = \frac{-6}{3} = 2$ $y - 5 = -2(x - 2)$	Two **wrongs** and a **right**

ADDITIONAL EXAMPLES

ALGEBRA

Examples 1 to 16 contain algebra content. Remind students that the same algebra problem or graph is presented three times, with one solution process correct but two incorrect. Ask students to find the correct solution and determine the incorrect steps and the reason for them in the others.

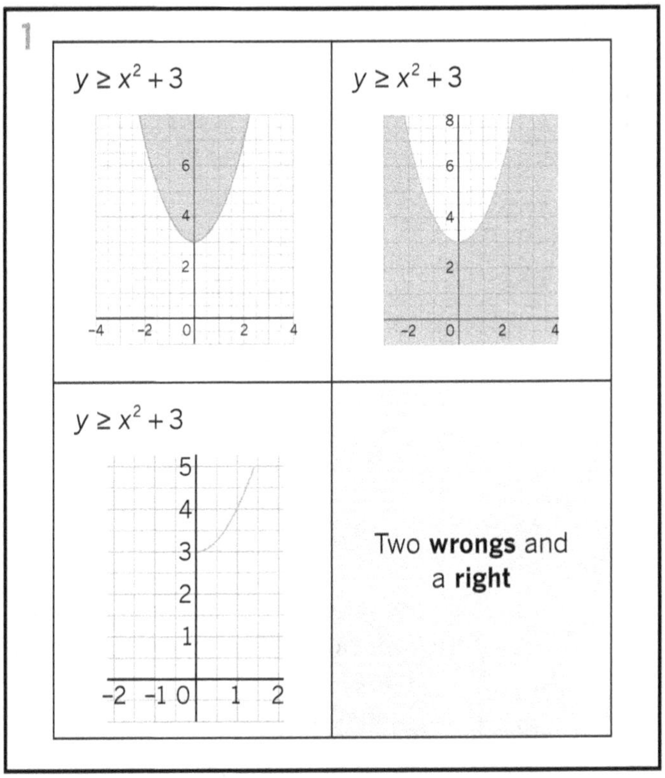

1. - Top left: The student put the shading in the wrong location.
   - Top right: Correct.
   - Bottom left: The student graphed only the positive domain of the function (due to the ≥) instead of graphing the full function and shading correctly.

NOTES

2

Solve the multi-step equation: $4(-x-2)-5=13$ $-4x+8-5=13$ $-4x+3=13$ $-4x=10$ $x=\frac{-10}{4}=\frac{-5}{2}$	Solve the multi-step equation: $4(-x-2)-5=13$ $-4x-8-5=13$ $-4x-13=13$ $-4x=0$ $x=0$
Solve the multi-step equation: $4(-x-2)-5=13$ $-4x-8-5=13$ $-4x-13=13$ $-4x=26$ $x=\frac{-26}{4}=\frac{-13}{2}$	Two **wrongs** and a **right**

2. • Top left: Distributed the 4 incorrectly in the first step.
   • Top right: In the fourth line, did not add 13 to both sides.
   • Bottom left: Correct.

3

Solve the absolute value inequality: $\lvert x+5\rvert < 15$ $-15 < x+5 < 15$ $-20 > x > 10$	Solve the absolute value inequality: $\lvert x+5\rvert < 15$ $-15 < x+5 < 15$ $-20 < x < 10$
Solve the absolute value inequality: $\lvert x+5\rvert < 15$ $-15 < x+5 < 15$ $-20 < x < 20$	Two **wrongs** and a **right**

3. • Top left: In last step, when subtracting 5 from both sides, the inequality signs do NOT change.
   • Top right: Correct.
   • Bottom left: In last step, when subtracting 5 from both sides, incorrectly arrived at 20 (15 – 5 – 10).

4

Find the slope of the line that passes through (−2, 5) and (−2, 1). $m=\frac{5-1}{-2-2}=\frac{4}{-4}=-1$	Find the slope of the line that passes through (−2, 5) and (−2, 1). $m=\frac{5-1}{-2--2}=\frac{4}{0}$ Slope is undefined
Find the slope of the line that passes through (−2, 5) and (−2, 1). $m=\frac{-2--2}{5-1}=\frac{0}{4}=0$	Two **wrongs** and a **right**

4. - Top left: The denominator is incorrect. Should be −2 − (−2).
   - Top right: Correct.
   - Bottom left: Subtracted the *x*-coordinates in the numerator and the *y*-coordinates in the denominator.

5

Given $f(x)=5x-2$, find the value of *x* when $f(x)=8$. $f(8)=5(8)-2$ $f(8)=38$	Given $f(x)=5x-2$, find the value of *x* when $f(x)=8$. $f(8)=5(8)-2$ $f(8)=38$ $f=4.75$
Given $f(x)=5x-2$, find the value of *x* when $f(x)=8$. $8=5x-2$ $10=5x$ $2=x$	Two **wrongs** and a **right**

5. - Top left: Incorrectly substituted 8 for *x*. We do not know the value of *x*. We only know that $f(x)=8$.
   - Top right: Solved for *f* in the last step; *f* is not a variable.
   - Bottom left: Correct.

6

$(x-3)^2-5=11$ $(x-3)^2=16$ $x-3=4$ $x=7$	$(x-3)^2-5=11$ $(x-3)^2=16$ $x-3=\pm4$ $x=3\pm4$ $x=7$ or $x=-1$
$(x-3)^2-5=11$ $(x-3)^2=6$ $x-3=\pm6$ $x=3\pm6$ $x=9$ or $x=-3$	Two **wrongs** and a **right**

6. - Top left: When taking the square root of both sides of an equation, you need to consider both the positive and negative root.
   - Top right: Correct.
   - Bottom left: First step incorrect; need to add 5 to both sides.

7

Simplify the expression: $\frac{2(3)(2x+6)}{6}$ $\frac{6(6x+18)}{6}$ $6x+18$	Simplify the expression: $\frac{2(3)(2x+6)}{6}$ $\frac{2(6x+18)}{6}$ $2(x+18)$ $2x+36$
Simplify the expression: $\frac{2(3)(2x+6)}{6}$ $\frac{6(2x+6)}{6}$ $2x+6$	Two **wrongs** and a **right**

7. - Top left: Distributed the 3 twice.
   - Top right: Incorrectly divided $\frac{(6x+18)}{6}$. It should yield $x + 3$.
   - Bottom left: Correct.

8

$\frac{y^3x^{-2}}{y^{-4}x^3}$ $\frac{y^3y^4}{x^2x^3}$ $\frac{y^{12}}{x^6}$	$\frac{y^3x^{-2}}{y^{-4}x^3}$ $\frac{y^3y^4}{x^2x^3}$ $\frac{y^7}{x^5}$
$\frac{y^3x^{-2}}{y^{-4}x^3}$ $\frac{y^7}{x^1}$ $\frac{1}{x^1y^7}$	Two **wrongs** and a **right**

8. - Top left: Incorrectly multiplied x^2x^3.
   - Top right: Correct.
   - Bottom left: Exponent of x variable is incorrect in first step. Student probably added the exponents 3 + (−2) instead of subtracting.

9

$\lvert -3-4\rvert + \lvert -6+1\rvert$ $\lvert -7\rvert + \lvert -5\rvert$ 7 + 5 12	$\lvert -3-4\rvert + \lvert -6+1\rvert$ $\lvert 3+4\rvert + \lvert 6+1\rvert$ 7 + 7 14
$\lvert -3-4\rvert + \lvert -6+1\rvert$ $\lvert -1\rvert + \lvert -5\rvert$ 1 + 5 6	Two **wrongs** and a **right**

9. - Top left: Correct.
   - Top right: Incorrect first step. Should first add/subtract the numbers inside the absolute values.
   - Bottom left: $\lvert -3-4\rvert = \lvert -7\rvert$.

10

$x^2 - 5x + 6 = 2$ $(x - 3)(x - 2) = 2$ $x - 3 = 2$ or $x - 2 = 2$ $x = 5$ or $x = 4$	$x^2 - 5x + 6 = 2$ $x^2 - 5x + 4 = 0$ $(x + 4)(x + 1) = 0$ $x + 4 = 0$ or $x + 1 = 0$ $x = -4$ or $x = -1$
$x^2 - 5x + 6 = 2$ $x^2 - 5x + 4 = 0$ $(x - 4)(x - 1) = 0$ $x - 4 = 0$ or $x - 1 = 0$ $x = 4$ or $x = 1$	Two **wrongs** and a **right**

10.
- Top left: First step incorrect. Need to be sure that equation = 0.
- Top right: Factored incorrectly.
- Bottom left: Correct.

11

$\frac{x}{2}+\frac{x}{3}=6$ $3x+2x=36$ $5x=36$ $x=\frac{36}{5}$	$\frac{x}{2}+\frac{x}{3}=6$ $3x+2x=6$ $5x=6$ $x=\frac{6}{5}$
$\frac{x}{2}+\frac{x}{3}=6$ $\frac{3x}{6}+\frac{2x}{6}=6$ $\frac{5x}{6}=6$ $5x=36$ $x=\frac{5}{36}$	Two **wrongs** and a **right**

11.
- Top left: Correct.
- Top right: Did not correctly multiply right-hand side of equation by 6.
- Bottom left: Last step incorrect. Should have divided both sides by 5.

12

Parabola with vertex (2, –3)

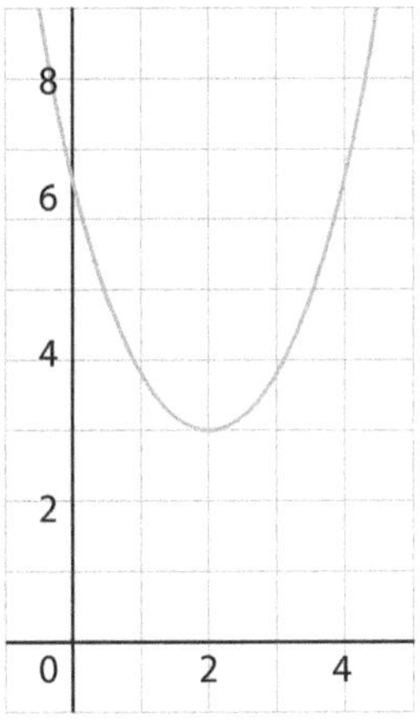

Parabola with vertex (2, –3)

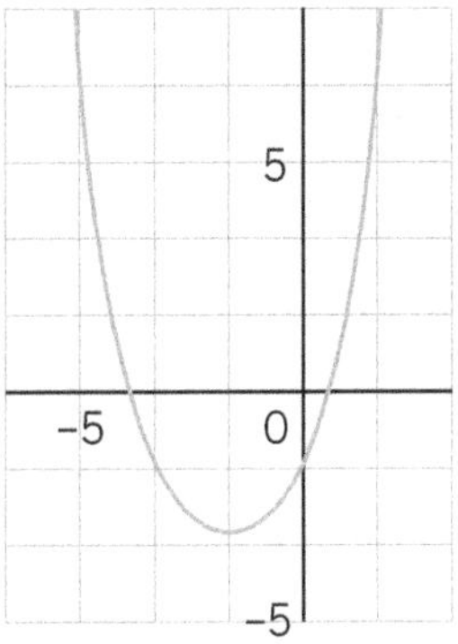

Parabola with vertex (2, –3)

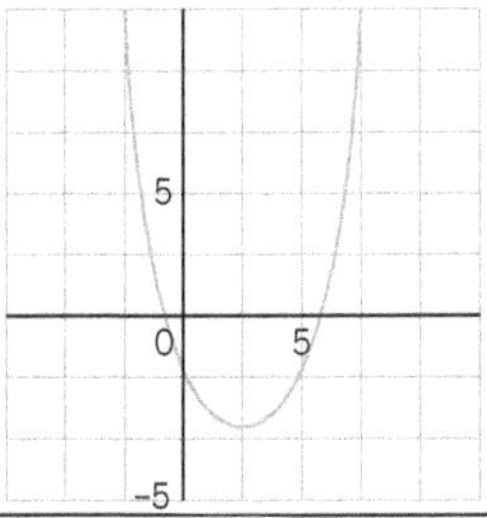

Two **wrongs** and a **right**

12. • Top left: Vertex is (2, 3).
 • Top right: Vertex is (–2, –3).
 • Bottom left: Correct.

NOTES

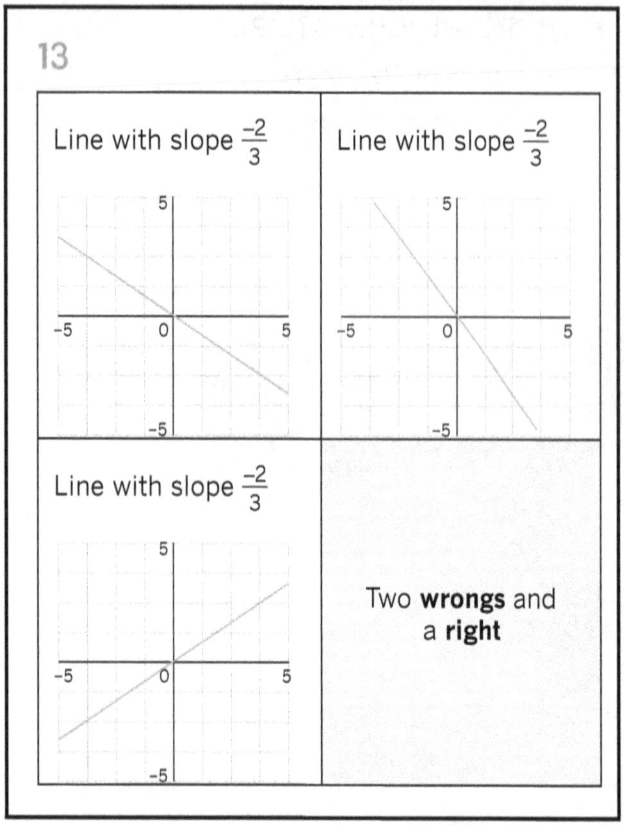

13.
- Top left: Correct.
- Top right: Slope is $\frac{-3}{2}$.
- Bottom left: Slope is $\frac{2}{3}$.

NOTES

14

Line graphed is ⊥ to $y = 3x+1$

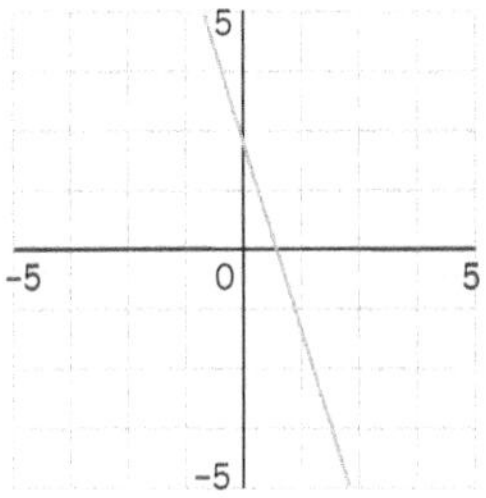

Line graphed is ⊥ to $y = 3x+1$

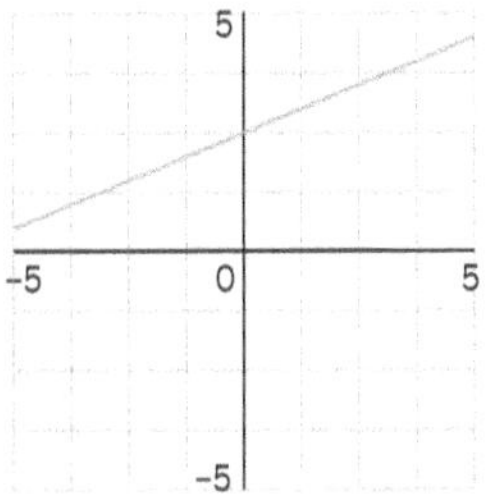

Line graphed is ⊥ to $y = 3x+1$

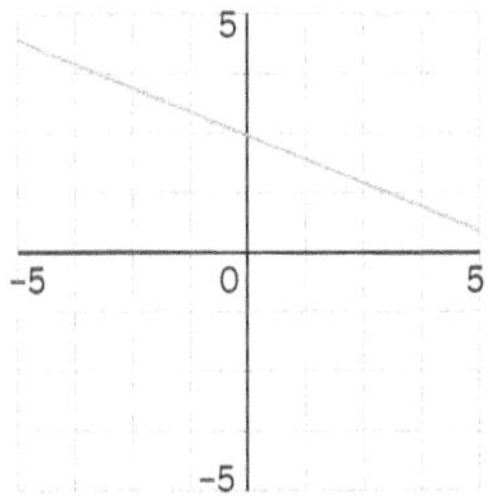

Two **wrongs** and a **right**

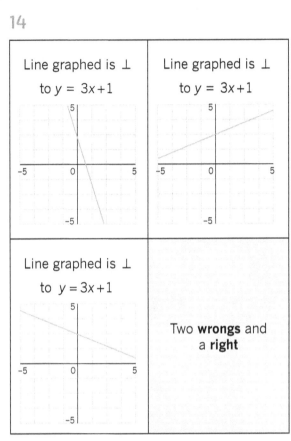

14.
- Top left: Slope is −3.
- Top right: Slope is $\frac{1}{3}$.
- Bottom left: Correct.

NOTES

15

Graph of

$y = 2(x-3)^2 - 5$

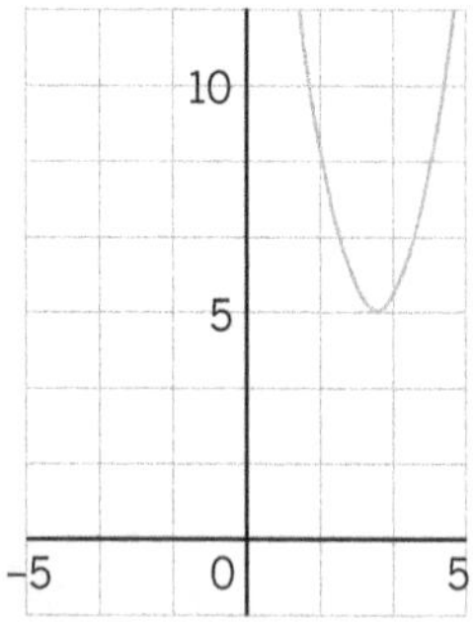

Graph of

$y = 2(x-3)^2 - 5$

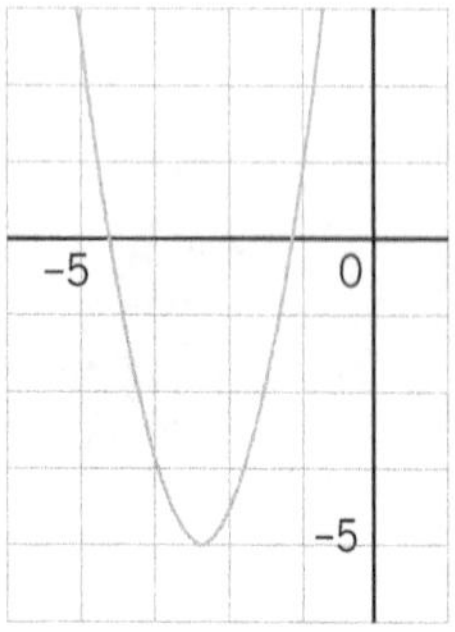

Graph of

$y = 2(x-3)^2 - 5$

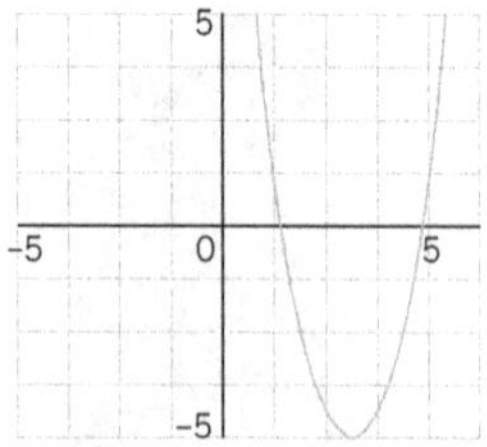

Two **wrongs** and a **right**

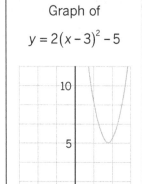

15. - Top left: Graph of $y = 2(x-3)^2 + 5$.
    - Top right: Graph of $y = 2(x+3)^2 - 5$.
    - Bottom left: Correct.

NOTES

16

Graph of $y = 5\left(\frac{1}{3}\right)^x$

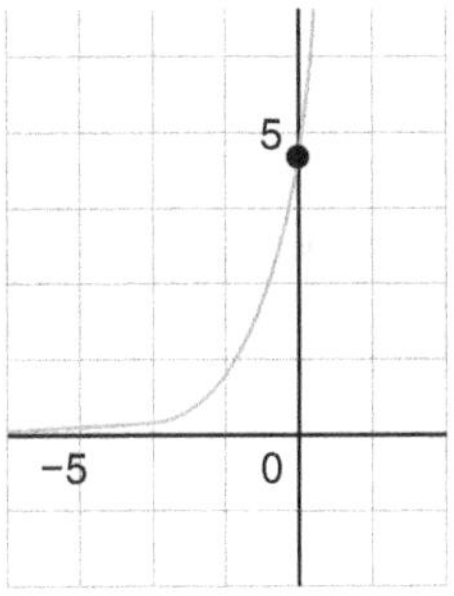

Graph of $y = 5\left(\frac{1}{3}\right)^x$

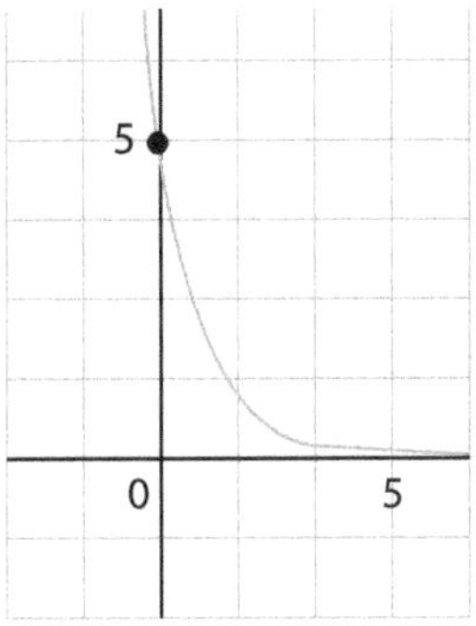

Graph of $y = 5\left(\frac{1}{3}\right)^x$

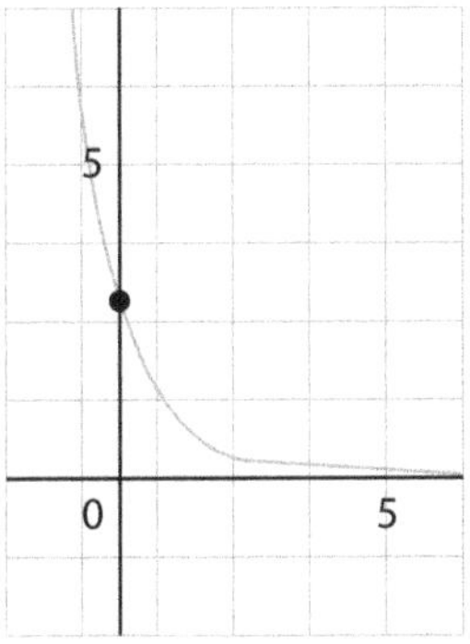

Two **wrongs** and a **right**

16.
- Top left: Graph of $y = 5(3)^x$.
- Top right: Correct.
- Bottom left: Graph of $y = 3\left(\frac{1}{3}\right)^x$.

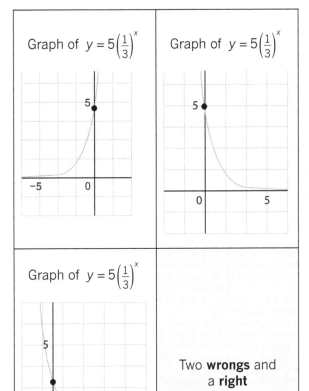

NOTES

GEOMETRY

The next set of examples (17–29) contains geometry content. The routine premise is the same, with two incorrect solutions and one correct.

17

Points B and D are tangent to the circle.

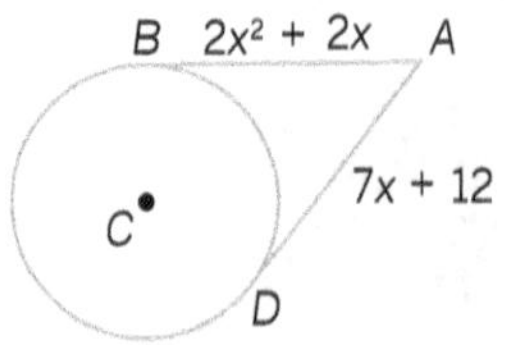

$2x^2 + 2x = 7x + 12$
$2x^2 - 5x - 12 = 0$
$(2x + 3)(x - 4) = 0$
$2x = -3$ or $x = 4$
$x = \frac{-3}{2}$ or $x = 4$

Points B and D are tangent to the circle.

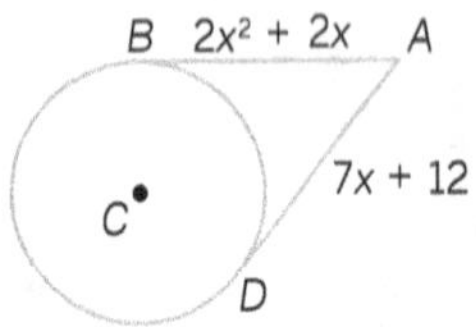

$2x^2 + 2x = 7x + 12$
$2x^2 - 5x - 12 = 0$
$(2x + 3)(x - 4) = 0$
$2x = -3$ or $x = 4$
$x = 4$

Points B and D are tangent to the circle.

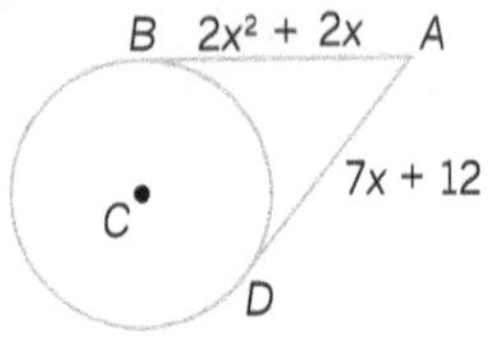

$2x^2 + 2x = 7x + 12$
$2x^2 - 5x - 12 = 0$
$(2x - 3)(x + 4) = 0$
$2x = 3$ or $x = -4$
$x = \frac{3}{2}$

Two **wrongs** and a **right**

17.
- Top left: Correct.
- Top right: Eliminated the negative solution, but in fact the solution is possible.
- Bottom left: Factored incorrectly.

18

SU is the diameter of the circle. Find the $m\widehat{ST}$.	SU is the diameter of the circle. Find the $m\widehat{ST}$.

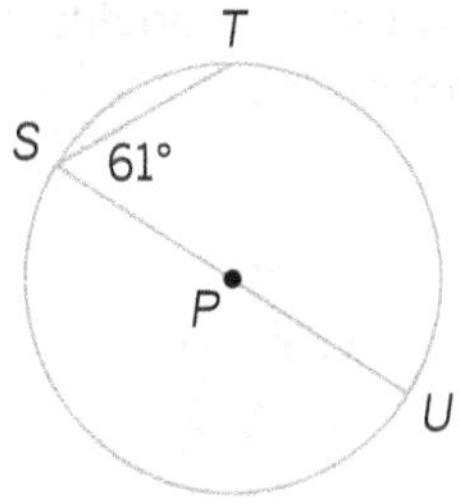

$m\widehat{ST} = 61$

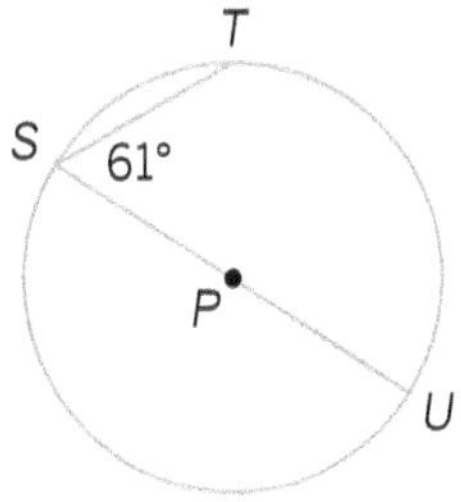

$m\widehat{TU} = 2(61) = 122$

$m\widehat{ST} = 122$

SU is the diameter of the circle. Find the $m\widehat{ST}$.

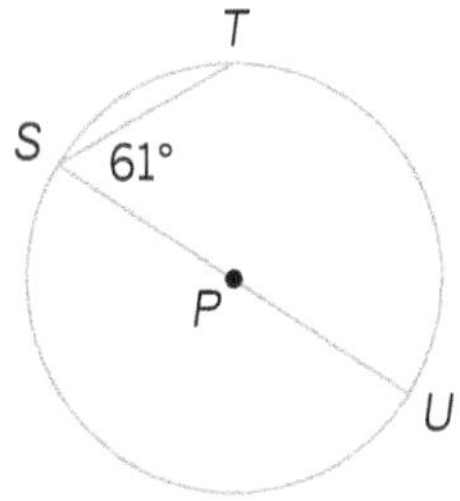

$m\widehat{TU} = 2(61) = 122$

$m\widehat{ST} = 180 - 122 = 58$

Two **wrongs** and a **right**

18.
- Top left: Incorrectly assumed that the angle TSU = $m\widehat{ST}$.
- Top right: Correctly found $m\widehat{TU}$, but $m\widehat{TU}$ does not equal $m\widehat{ST}$.
- Bottom left: Correct.

NOTES

19

Top left

Solve for x.

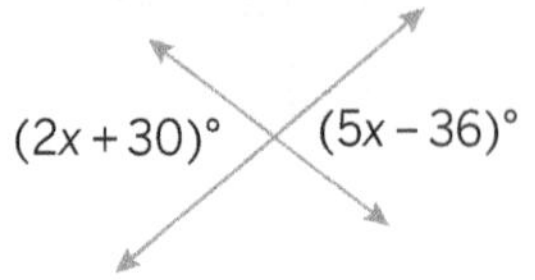

$$2x + 30 = 5x - 36$$
$$66 = 3x$$
$$x = 22$$

Top right

Solve for x.

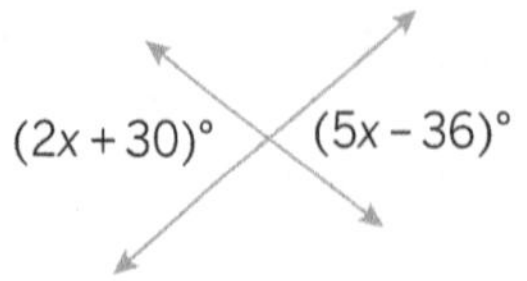

$$2x + 30 = 5x - 36 = 180$$
$$7x - 66 = 180$$
$$7x = 186$$
$$x = \frac{186}{7}$$

Bottom left

Solve for x.

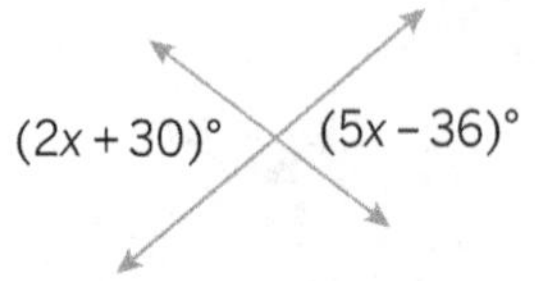

$$2x + 30 + 5x - 36 = 90$$
$$7x - 6 = 90$$
$$7x = 96$$
$$x = \frac{96}{7}$$

Bottom right

Two **wrongs** and a **right**

19.
- Top left: Correct.
- Top right: Incorrectly assumed that the angles were supplementary.
- Bottom left: Incorrectly assumed that the angles were complementary.

NOTES

20

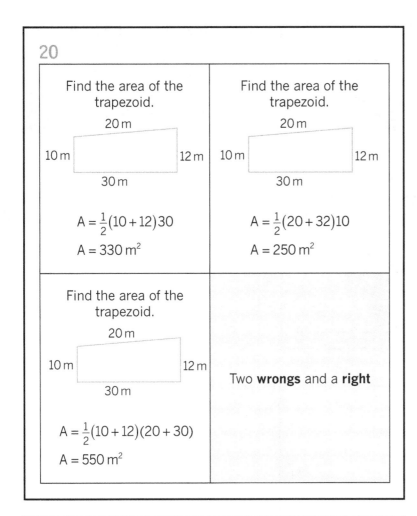

Find the area of the trapezoid. 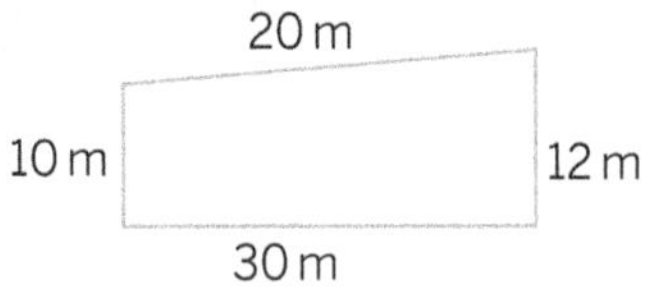 $A = \frac{1}{2}(10+12)30$ $A = 330\text{ m}^2$	Find the area of the trapezoid. 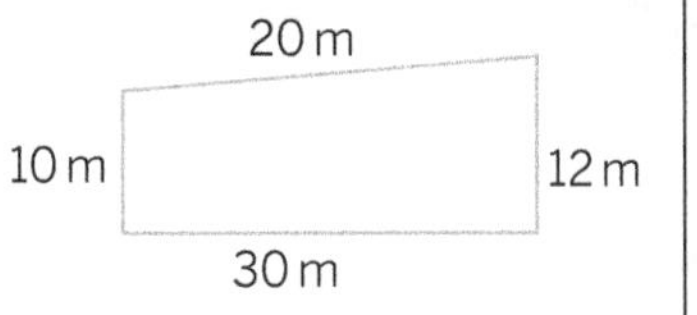 $A = \frac{1}{2}(20+32)10$ $A = 250\text{ m}^2$
Find the area of the trapezoid. 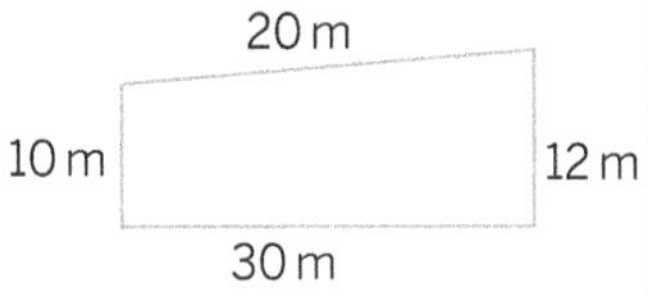 $A = \frac{1}{2}(10+12)(20+30)$ $A = 550\text{ m}^2$	Two **wrongs** and a **right**

20.
- Top left: Correct.
- Top right: Incorrectly assumed the bases were 20 and 30.
- Bottom left: Did not identify the height correctly.

21

Find the volume of the cylinder. 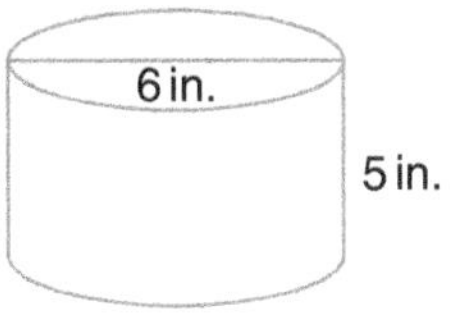 $V = \pi(5)^2 6 = 150\pi$	Find the volume of the cylinder. 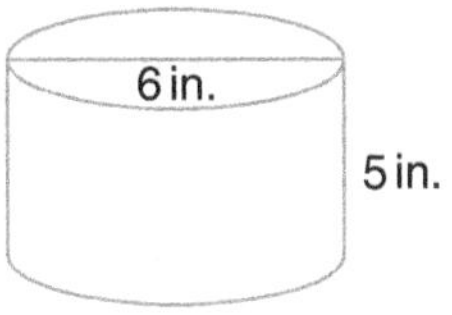 $V = \pi(6)^2 5 = 180\pi$
Find the volume of the cylinder. 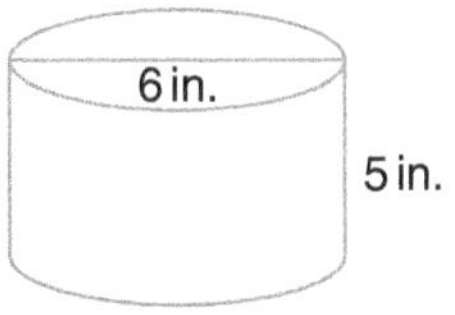 $V = \pi(3)^2 5 = 45\pi$	Two **wrongs** and a **right**

21.
- Top left: Radius is not 5.
- Top right: Radius is not 6.
- Bottom left: Correct.

22

Angles A and B are supplementary. $m\angle A = 36$; find $m\angle B$. $36 + m\angle B = 90$ $m\angle B = 54$	Angles A and B are supplementary. $m\angle A = 36$; find $m\angle B$. $36 + m\angle B = 180$ $m\angle B = 144$
Angles A and B are supplementary. $m\angle A = 36$; find $m\angle B$. $36 + m\angle B = 360$ $m\angle B = 324$	Two **wrongs** and a **right**

22.
- Top left: Used the definition of complementary angles.
- Top right: Correct.
- Bottom left: Used 360 instead of 180 degrees.

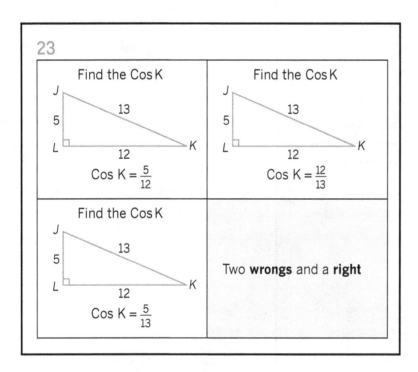

23

Find the Cos K

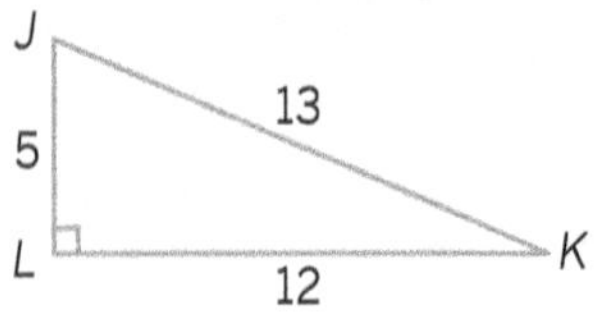

Cos K = $\frac{5}{12}$

Find the Cos K

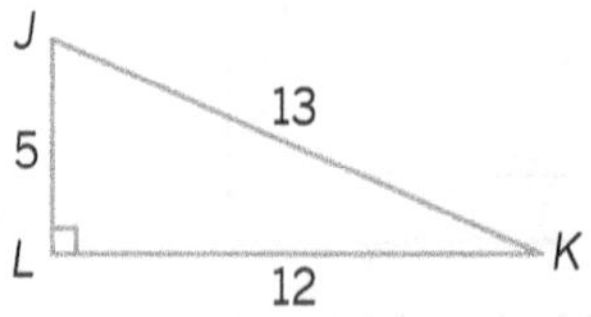

Cos K = $\frac{12}{13}$

Find the Cos K

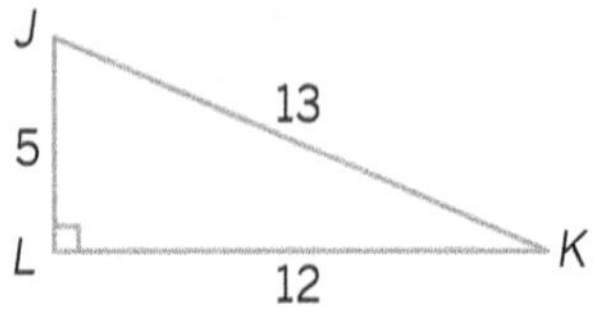

Cos K = $\frac{5}{13}$

Two **wrongs** and a **right**

23.
- Top left: Incorrectly used opposite/adjacent (which would be the Tan K).
- Top right: Correct.
- Bottom left: Incorrectly used opposite side/hypotenuse (which would be the Sin K).

24

Find the $m\angle MBD$.

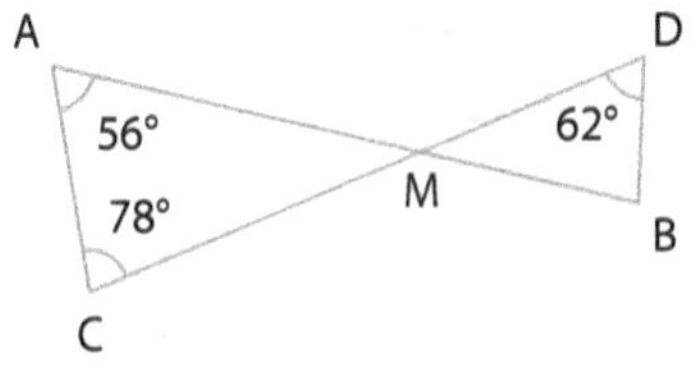

$180 - (56 + 78)$
$180 - 134$
46

Find the $m\angle MBD$.

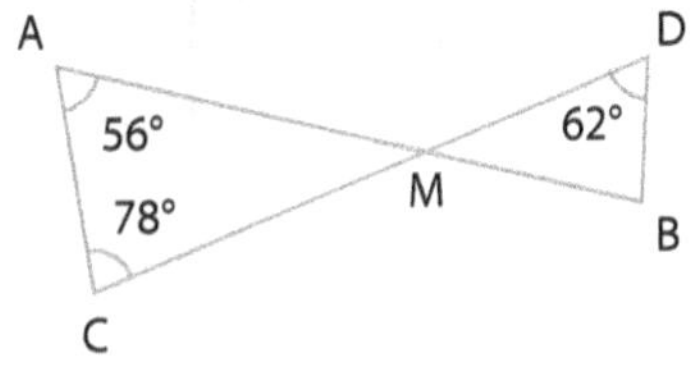

Triangle MBD is isosceles, and thus, $m\angle MBD = m\angle MDB = 62$.

Find the $m\angle MBD$.

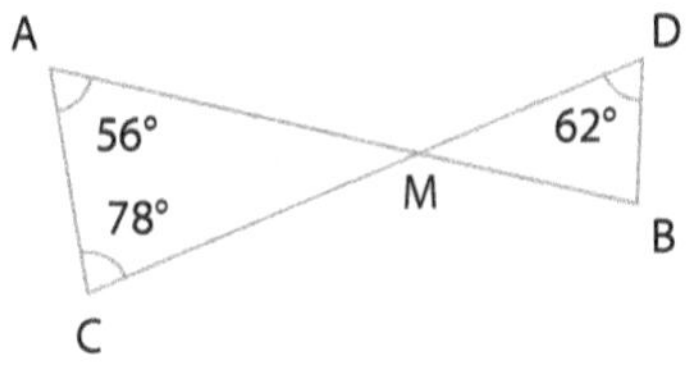

$m\angle AMC = 180 - (56 + 78)$

$m\angle AMC = 46$

$m\angle AMC = m\angle DMB = 46$

$m\angle MDB = 180 - (46 + 62)$

$m\angle MDB = 180 - (108)$

$m\angle MDB = 72$

Two **wrongs** and a **right**

24.
- Top left: Found the $m\angle AMC$.
- Top right: We do not know that Triangle MBD is isosceles.
- Bottom left: Correct.

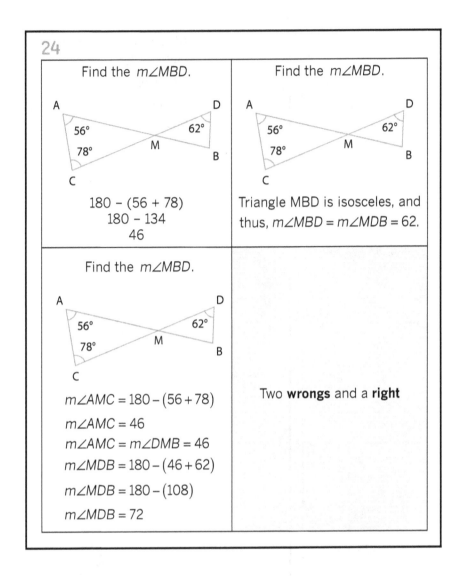

NOTES

25

The rectangle has area = 432 and has 12 congruent squares. What is the perimeter?

Let the side of one of the small squares = x. Thus

$$(4x)(3x) = 432.$$
$$12x^2 = 432$$
$$x^2 = 36$$
$$x = 6$$

Perimeter $= 6 \times 4 = 24$

The rectangle has area = 432 and has 12 congruent squares. What is the perimeter?

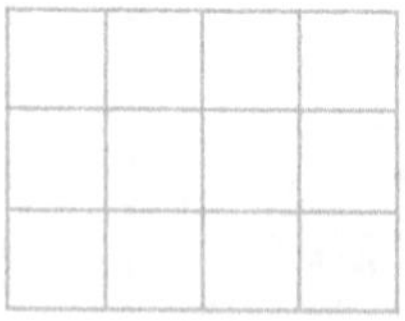

Let the side of one of the small squares = x. Thus

$$(4x)(3x) = 432.$$
$$12x^2 = 432$$
$$x^2 = 36$$
$$x = 6$$

Perimeter $= 6 \times 14 = 84$

The rectangle has area = 432 and has 12 congruent squares. What is the perimeter?

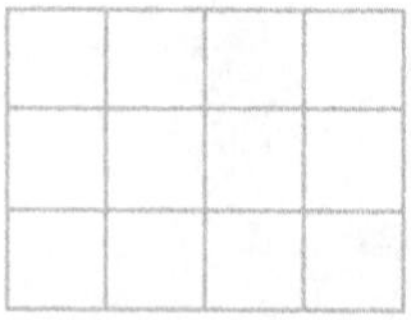

It is NOT possible to find the perimeter.

Two **wrongs** and a **right**

25.
- Top left: The last step is incorrect as the length of the small square is 6.
- Top right: Correct.
- Bottom left: It is possible to find the perimeter.

26

ABC is a right triangle.
$AM \perp BC$.
$m\angle ABC = 55$.
Find $m\angle MAC$.

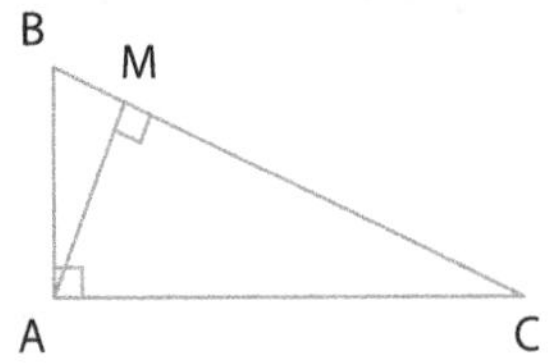

$m\angle ABC + m\angle ACM + 90° = 180°$

$m\angle ACM = 180 - 90 - 55 = 35°$

$m\angle MAC + m\angle ACM + 90 = 180°$

$m\angle MAC = 180 - 90 - m\angle ACM$

$= 180 - 90 - 55 = 35°$

ABC is a right triangle.
$AM \perp BC$.
$m\angle ABC = 55$.
Find $m\angle MAC$.

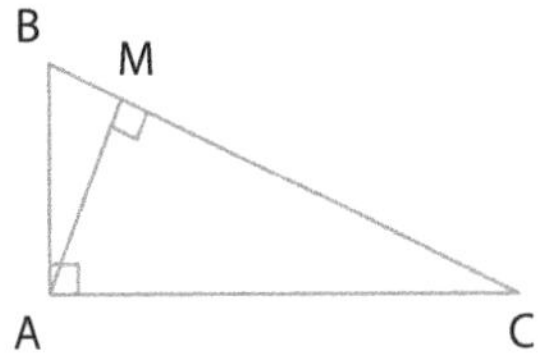

$m\angle ABC + m\angle ACM + 90 = 180°$

$m\angle ACM = 180 - 90 - 55 = 45°$

$m\angle MAC + m\angle ACM + 90 = 180°$

$m\angle MAC = 180 - 90 - m\angle ACM$

$= 108 - 90 - 45 = 45°$

ABC is a right triangle.
$AM \perp BC$.
$m\angle ABC = 55$.
Find $m\angle MAC$.

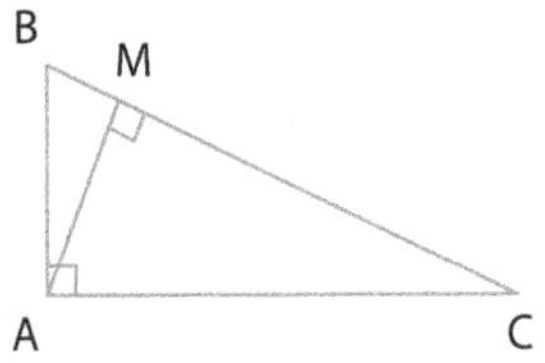

$m\angle ABC + m\angle ACM + 90 = 180°$

$m\angle ACM = 180 - 90 - 55 = 35°$

$m\angle MAC + m\angle ACM + 90 = 180°$

$m\angle MAC = 180 - 90 - m\angle ACM$

$= 180 - 90 - 35 = 55°$

Two **wrongs** and a **right**

26.
- Top left: Substitution of 55 for $m\angle ACM$ is incorrect.
- Top right: Incorrect computation of 180 - 90 - 55.
- Bottom left: Correct.

27

Parallelogram WXYZ is mapped to its image W'X'Y'Z' by a reflection across the *x*-axis.

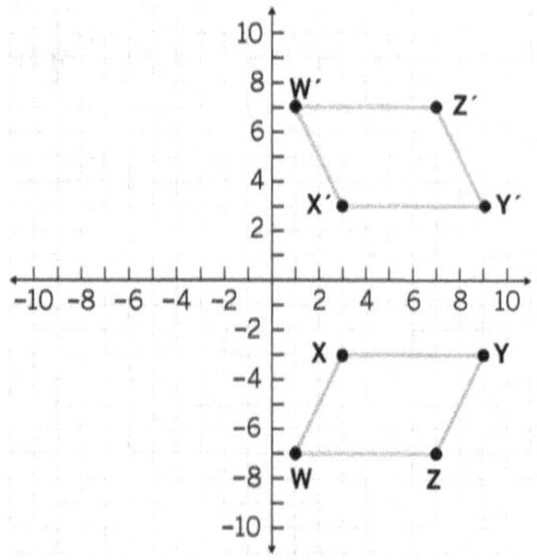

Parallelogram WXYZ is mapped to its image W'X'Y'Z' by a reflection across the *x*-axis.

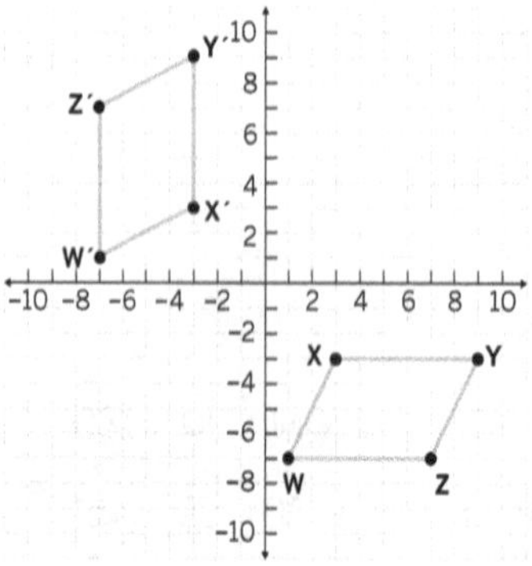

Parallelogram WXYZ is mapped to its image W'X'Y'Z' by a reflection across the *x*-axis.

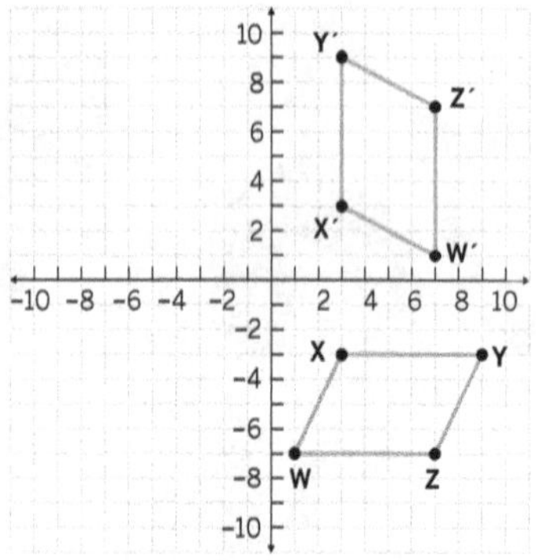

Two **wrongs** and a **right**

27.
- Top left: Correct.
- Top right: Shows a reflection across the line $y = x$.
- Bottom left: Shows a 90° counterclockwise rotation about the origin.

28

The following triangles are congruent by ASA. 	The following triangles are congruent by ASA. 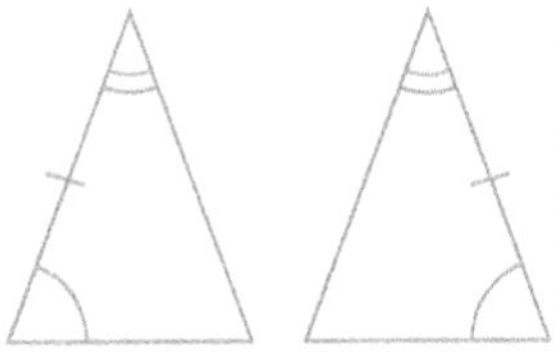
The following triangles are congruent by ASA. 	Two **wrongs** and a **right**

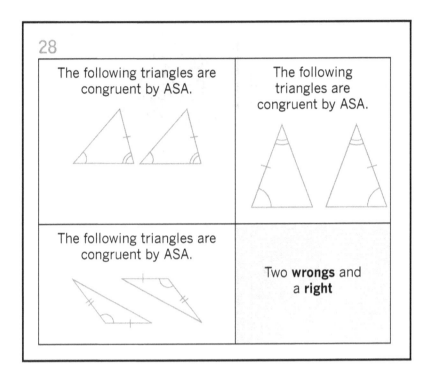

28.
- Top left: The triangles are congruent by AAS.
- Top right: Correct.
- Bottom left: The triangles are congruent by SAS.

NOTES

29

In ΔABC, $AC \parallel A'C'$. Find the length (y) of BC'.

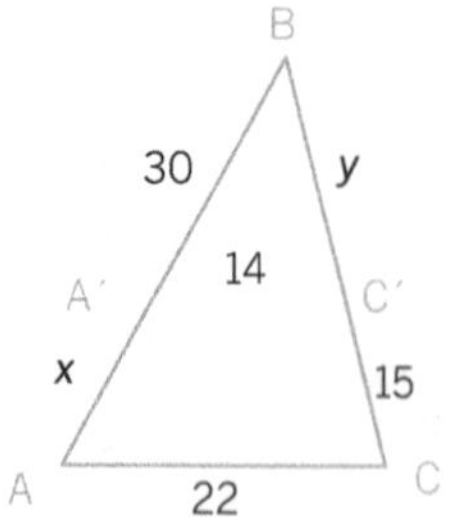

$$\frac{22}{14} = \frac{y+15}{y}$$

$$22y = 14(y+15)$$

$$22y = 14y + 210$$

$$8y = 210$$

$$y = 26.25$$

In ΔABC, $AC \parallel A'C'$. Find the length (y) of BC'.

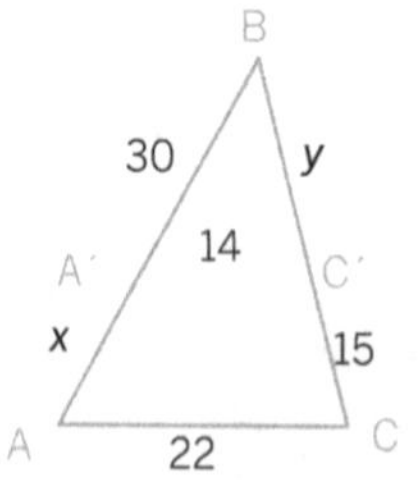

$$\frac{14}{30} = \frac{y}{y+15}$$

$$30y = 14(y+15)$$

$$30y = 14y + 210$$

$$16y = 210$$

$$y = 13.125$$

In ΔABC, $AC \parallel A'C'$. Find the length (y) of BC'.

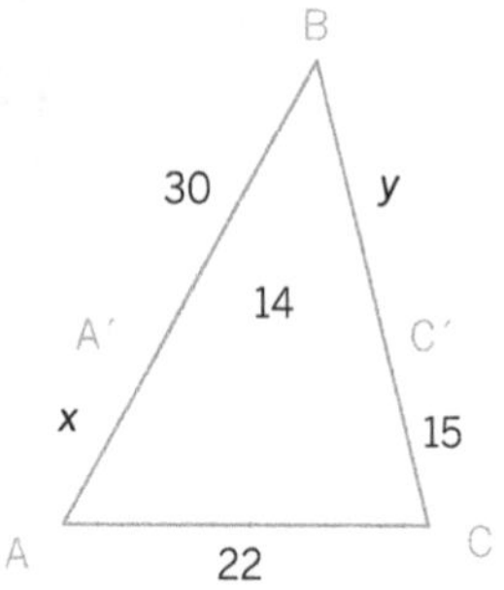

$$\frac{22}{14} = \frac{15}{y}$$

$$22y = 210$$

$$y = 9.54$$

Two **wrongs** and a **right**

29.
- Top left: Correct.
- Top right: Incorrect proportion.
- Bottom left: Incorrect proportion.

ROUTINE 5

A OR B

ABOUT THE ROUTINE

In this routine, students must be able to compare two different quantities and determine if they are equal, if one is larger than the other, or if inadequate information is provided to make the determination. This routine asks students to compare two quantities—Quantity A and Quantity B—and then determine which of the following statements describes the comparison:

- Quantity A is greater.
- Quantity B is greater.
- The two quantities are equal.
- The relationship cannot be determined from the information given.

Students should not waste time performing needless computations in order to compare the two quantities.

Column A	Column B
x is a positive number	
x	x^2

If one or both of the quantities are algebraic expressions, you can substitute easy numbers for the variables and compare the resulting quantities in your analysis. Consider all kinds of appropriate numbers before you give an answer: e.g., zero, positive and negative numbers, small and large numbers, fractions and decimals. If you see that Quantity A is greater than Quantity B in one case and Quantity B is greater than Quantity A in another case, choose "The relationship cannot be determined from the information given."

WHY IT MATTERS

In this routine, students must

- reason quickly and accurately about the relative sizes of two quantities, and
- engage in logical and numerical analysis and perceive that, in some cases, not enough information is provided to make such a decision.

Such reasoning is crucial in the development of mathematical sense making and should be the first step in almost all mathematics problems. Moreover, this routine highlights Mathematical Practice 2 (reason abstractly and quantitatively) and Mathematical Practice 7 (look for and make use of structure).

online resources All tasks can be downloaded for your use at resources.corwin.com/jumpstartroutines/highschool

WHAT THEY SHOULD UNDERSTAND FIRST

Students must first understand the conceptual underpinning of the example. The content of the examples will draw from algebra, geometry, and algebra II. Sufficient content knowledge of the given is necessary for students to explore the problems.

WHAT TO DO

1. Display the given information and the two quantities in Columns A and B.
2. Have students work in pairs to determine if Quantity A is greater, Quantity B is greater, the two quantities are equal, or the relationship cannot be determined from the information given.
3. Facilitate student reflection and discussion.
4. Help students to think about simplifying, transforming, or estimating one or both of the given quantities only as much as is necessary to compare them. Plugging in numbers is one of the most effective strategies.

ANTICIPATED STRATEGIES FOR THIS EXAMPLE

In this example, most students will be quick to recognize that $x^2 > x$. Students must note, however, that this is only true if $x > 1$. If $x = 1$, then the two expressions are equivalent, and if $0 < x < 1$, then $x^2 < x$. Thus, the correct response is that the relationship cannot be determined from the information given.

Column A	Column B
x is a positive number	
x	x^2

NOTES

ADDITIONAL EXAMPLES

ALGEBRA

Examples 1 to 20 draw on content from numerical operations and algebra.

1

Which column is greater?	
Column A	Column B
x and y are positive integers $3x+6y=1{,}782{,}617$	
Maximum value of x	Maximum value of y

1. Column A is greater.

In this example, students use the fact that x and y are positive integers.

If $x=0$, then $6y=1{,}782{,}617$.

If $y=0$, then $3x=1{,}782{,}617$.

Thus, the maximum value of x would be larger than the maximum value of y.

2

Which column is greater?	
Column A	Column B
$7b-2c=12$ $3c-6b=3$	
$b+c$	14

2. Column A is greater.

In this example, students need to realize that they do NOT need to solve for b or c. They can merely add the two equations and arrive at $b+c=15$.

3

Which column is greater?	
Column A	Column B
$(4^3)^4$	$4^4 3^4$

3. Column A is greater.

$(4^3)^4 = 4^{12} = 16{,}777{,}216$

$4^4 3^4 = (4 \cdot 3)^4 = 12^4 = 20{,}736$

4

Which column is greater?	
Column A	Column B
The product of the integers from −10 to 5	The product of the integers from −5 to 10

4. Columns are equal.

Both lists of integers contain the number 0, so their products equal 0.

5

Which column is greater?	
Column A	Column B
$\frac{a}{b} < 0$	
ab	0

5. Column B is greater.

Given $\frac{a}{b} < 0$, either $a < 0$ or $b < 0$.

Thus, $ab < 0$.

6

Which column is greater?	
Column A	Column B
The degree of a quadratic polynomial	The degree of a cubic polynomial

6. Column B is greater.

The degree of a quadratic polynomial is 2.

The degree of a cubic polynomial is 3.

7

Which column is greater?	
Column A	Column B
x not equal to 0	
$(2x+4)(x+1)$	$2x^2+5x+4$

7. Not enough information.

$(2x+4)(x+1)=2x^2+6x+4$ and when compared to $2x^2+5x+4$, it is unknown which quantity is larger since we do not know if x is positive or negative.

8

Which column is greater?	
Column A	Column B
$a>b>0$	
$\frac{1}{a}$	$\frac{1}{b}$

8. Column B is greater.

It is given that $a>b>0$, so $a>0$ and $b>0$, and $a>b$.

For fractions with the same numerator, the smaller the denominator, the larger the value of the fraction.

9

Which column is greater?	
Column A	Column B
The slope of the line $2x+3y=7$	The slope of the line perpendicular to $2x+3y=7$

9. Column B is greater.

$2x+3y=7$ has a negative slope (see graph).

Thus, the line perpendicular to it must have a positive slope.

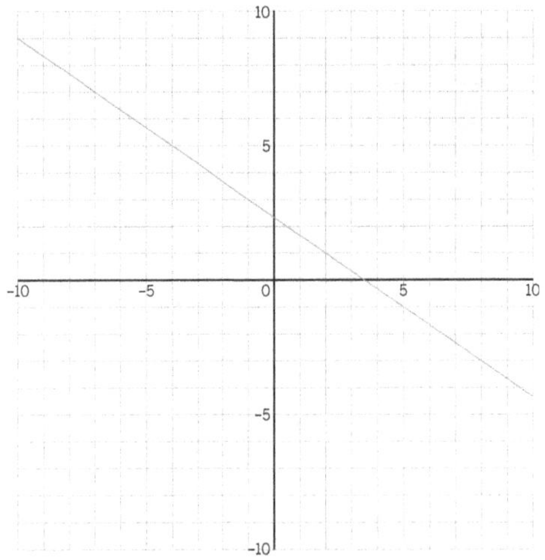

10

Which column is greater?	
Column A	Column B
Points $(4, y_1)$ and $(0, y_2)$ are on line l. The slope of line $l = \frac{3}{4}$	
$y_2 - y_1$	3

10. Column B is greater.

Since $(4, y_1)$ and $(0, y_2)$, then

$$\frac{y_2 - y_1}{0 - 4} = \frac{3}{4}$$

$$y_2 - y_1 = -3$$

Also see link to Desmos at https://tinyurl.com/yc9cafdx.

11

Which column is greater?	
Column A	Column B
x and y are not 0	
$(x+y)^2$	$x^2 + y^2$

11. Not enough information.

$$(x+y)^2 = x^2 + 2xy + y^2$$

$$x^2 + 2xy + y^2 > x^2 + y^2$$

only if $2xy > 0$.

We do not know if $xy > 0$ since x or y could be negative.

12

Which column is greater?	
Column A	Column B
$y > 0$	
$(y+1)(y)(y-1)$	y^3

12. Column B is greater.

$$(y+1)(y)(y-1) = (y+1)(y-1)y$$
$$= (y^2 - 1)y = y^3 - y$$

$y^3 - y < y^3$ since $y > 0$.

13

Which column is greater?	
Column A	Column B
$x \geq 1$	
x^{10}	x^{100}

13. Not enough information.

If $x = 1$, then both quantities yield 1.

If $x > 1$, then column B is larger.

14

Which column is greater?	
Column A	Column B
x is a positive integer > 1	
The number of distinct prime factors of x	The number of distinct prime factors of $2x$

14. Not enough information.

If $x = 2$, then column A has 1 distinct prime factor (2) and column B also has only one (2). If $x = 3$, then column A has 1 distinct prime factor (3) and column B has two distinct prime factors (2 and 3).

15

Which column is greater?	
Column A	Column B
$xy = 3$	
$x + y$	4

15. Not enough information.

$x = 1$ and $y = 3$ yields both columns equal.

$x = \frac{1}{3}$ and $y = 9$ yields column A larger.

16

Which column is greater?	
Column A	Column B
$x = 3.25$, $y = 4.25$	
The average of x, $y - 1$, $x + 1$, and 7	The average of 7, y, y, and 3.25

16. Column B is greater.

Note that $y = x + 1$ and that 7 is in each column. Change all values in terms of y.

Column A: Average of $y - 1$, $y - 1$, y, and 7

Column B: Average of y, y, $y - 1$, and 7

17

Which column is greater?	
Column A	Column B
$\lvert x - 2 \rvert$	$\lvert 2 - x \rvert$

17. The columns are equal.

The absolute value of opposites is the same number.

$x - 2$ is the opposite of $2 - x$. This can be shown by multiplying either expression by -1.

18

Which column is greater?	
Column A	Column B
$xy < 0 < -x$	
y	0

18. Column A is greater.

$xy < 0$ and x must be negative (since $0 < -x$), thus, $y > 0$.

19

Which column is greater?	
Column A	Column B
$.\overline{313}$	$.\overline{31}$

19. Column A is greater.

$.\overline{313} = .313313313\ldots$

$.\overline{31} = .313131313\ldots$

20

Which column is greater?	
Column A	Column B
$x > y > 0$	
x^2	y^2

20. Column A is greater.

If $x > y$, then $x^2 > y^2$ if and only if x and y are both positive.

GEOMETRY

Examples 21 to 30 draw on content from geometry. You may decide to supply appropriate formulas to students when working on these examples.

21

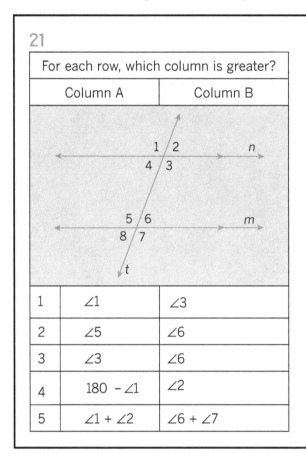

For each row, which column is greater?		
	Column A	Column B

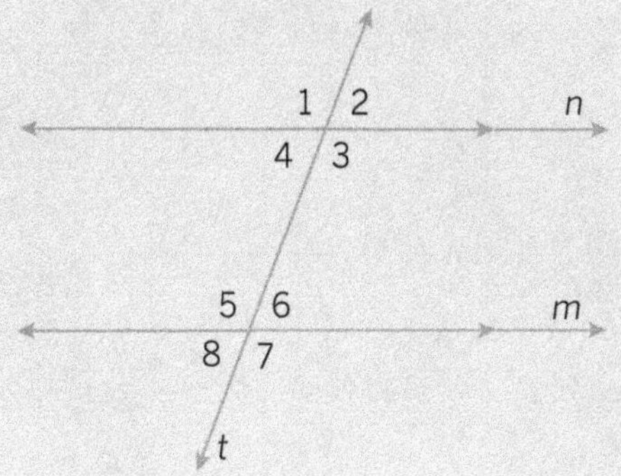

	Column A	Column B
1	$\angle 1$	$\angle 3$
2	$\angle 5$	$\angle 6$
3	$\angle 3$	$\angle 6$
4	$180 - \angle 1$	$\angle 2$
5	$\angle 1 + \angle 2$	$\angle 6 + \angle 7$

21. 1: Equal as $\angle 1 = \angle 3$.

2: Unknown as $\angle 5 + \angle 6 = 180$. If line t is perpendicular to line n, then $\angle 5 = \angle 6$.

3: Unknown as $\angle 3 + \angle 6 = 180$. If line t is perpendicular to line n, then $\angle 3 = \angle 6$.

4: Equal as $\angle 1 + \angle 2 = 180$

5: Equal as $\angle 1 + \angle 2 = 180$ and $\angle 6 + \angle 7 = 180$

22

Which column is greater?	
Column A	Column B
The sum of the interior angles of a regular pentagon	360 degrees

22. Column A is greater.

Sum of angles of a regular n-gon is $180(n - 2)$.

For a pentagon, $n = 5$, sum is $3 \times 180 = 540$.

23

Which column is greater?	
Column A	Column B
$x \geq 2$	
Rectangular prism with length = 6, width = 4, height = x	Cylinder with radius = x, height = x

23. Not enough information.

The volume of the rectangular prism = $4(6)x = 24x$.

The volume of a cylinder = $\pi r^2 h$, so the volume of the cylinder in column B = πx^3.

Graphing both functions for $x > 2$, we can see $24x > \pi x^3$ when $x = 2$ but not when $x = 3$.

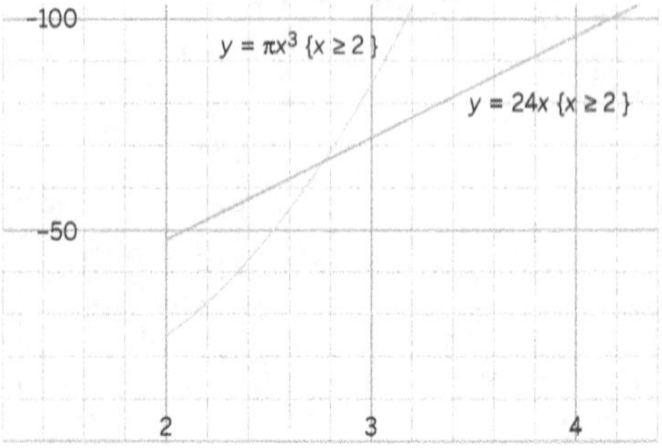

24

Which column is greater?	
Column A	Column B
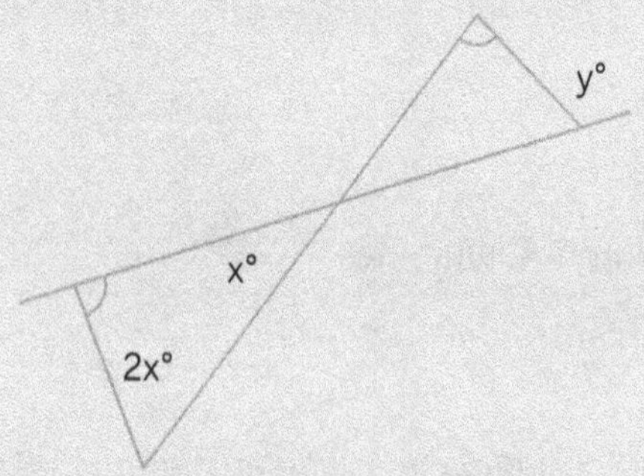	
4x	y

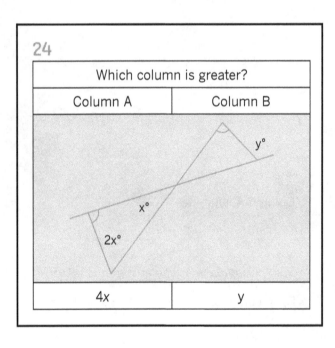

24. The columns are equal.

$x + 2x + 90 = 180$

$x = 30$

$(180 - y) + 90 + 30 = 180$

$y = 120$

25

Which column is greater?	
Column A	Column B
Triangle ABC is equilateral. 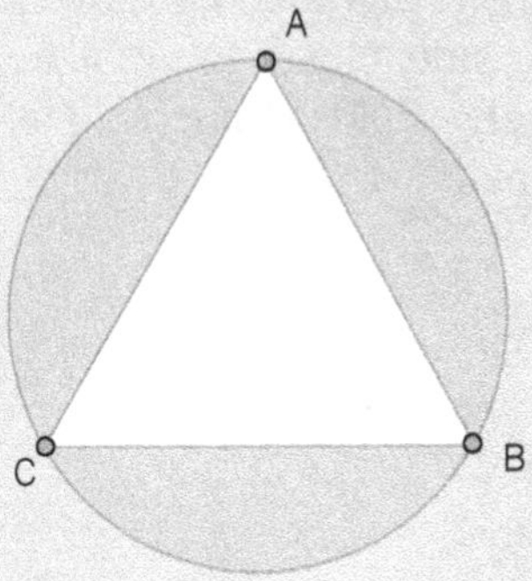	
Area of triangle ABC	Area of shaded region

25. Column B is greater.

First, draw the altitudes from each vertex of the equilateral triangle to the midpoint of the opposite side.

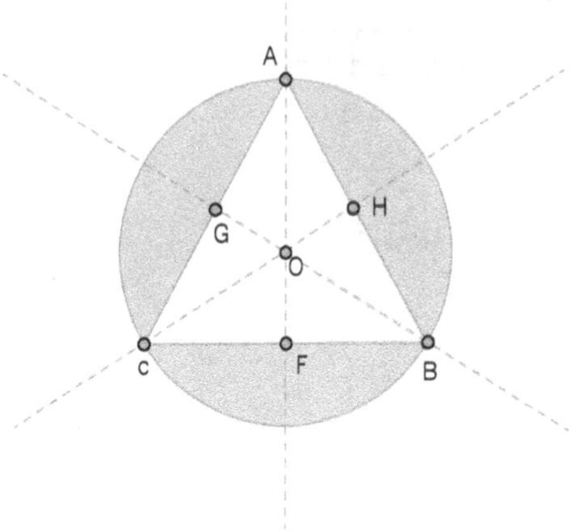

This will subdivide the equilateral triangle into six congruent 30-60-90 triangles, and OA, OB, and OC are all radii of the circle.

Assume r = 2. In 30-60-90 triangle FOB, the hypotenuse is OB = 2, so OF = 1. The remaining side, OB, opposite the 60°, must have a length of $\sqrt{3}$ and the area of triangle FOB $= \frac{1}{2}\sqrt{3}(1) = \frac{\sqrt{3}}{2}$. Six of these triangles make up the entire equilateral triangle, so the area of triangle

ABC $= 6\frac{\sqrt{3}}{2} = 3\sqrt{3} = 5.196$.

Given the circle with r = 2, then its area = 4π. The shaded area is $4\pi - 3\sqrt{3} = 7.37$.

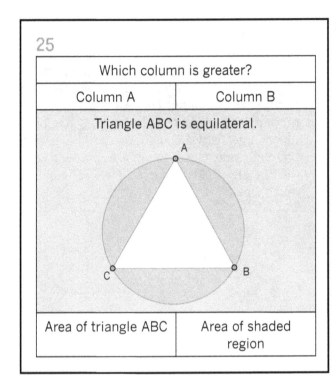

26

Which column is greater?	
Column A	Column B
In the diagram, O is the center of the circle and AB is a diameter.	
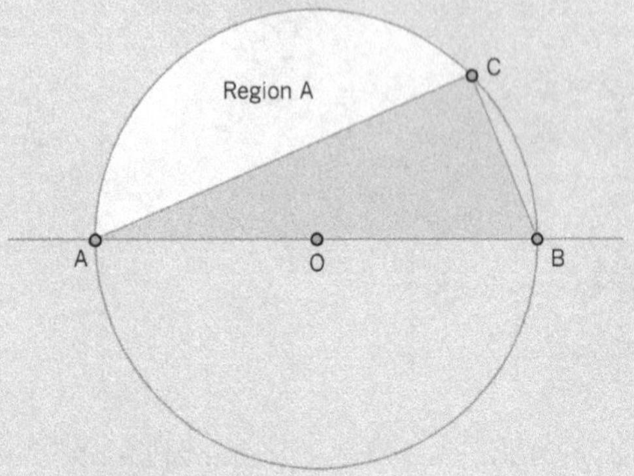	
Area of triangle ABC	Area of region A

26. Not enough information.

We know AB is a diameter, and we know that angle ACB is 90°. We don't know the position of point C. By moving point C around, we could change the situation. For example, we could move point C toward point B, making Region A much larger. Or we could move point C toward the other side, closer to point A, in which case the triangle would be much bigger and Region A much smaller.

27

Which column is greater?	
Column A	Column B
$AC > CB > AB$	
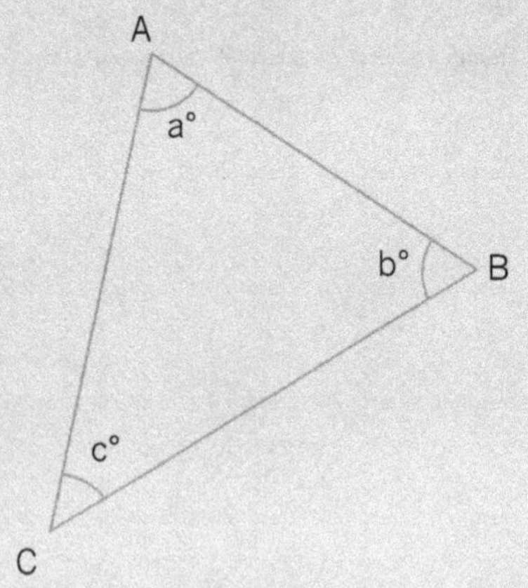	
a	b

27. Column B is greater.

The longest side of a triangle is opposite the largest angle. Thus, $b > a > c$.

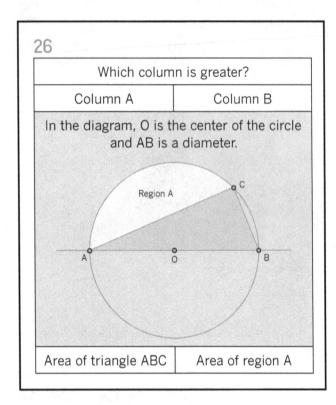

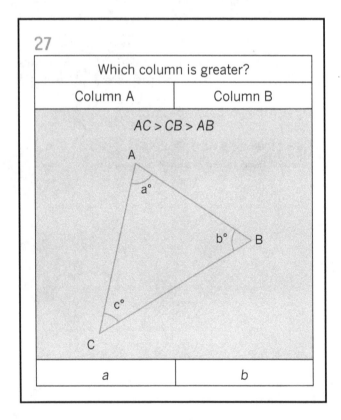

28

Which column is greater?	
Column A	Column B
The area of a square with a perimeter of 12.	The area of a parallelogram with a perimeter of 16.

28. Not enough information.

The square with a perimeter of 12 has a side length of 3 and thus an area of 9. Now consider first the square with a side length of 4; this is a parallelogram with a perimeter of 16 and an area of 16; its area is greater than the first square's. But let's say we chose the rectangle whose height was 1 and width was 7. This is also a parallelogram with a perimeter of 16, but its area is 7, which is less than 9.

29

Which column is greater?	
Column A	Column B
The diameter of circle O is the same as the length of a side of square S.	
The area of circle O	The area of square S

29. Column B is greater.

See figure below; the circle can clearly be slid inside the square.

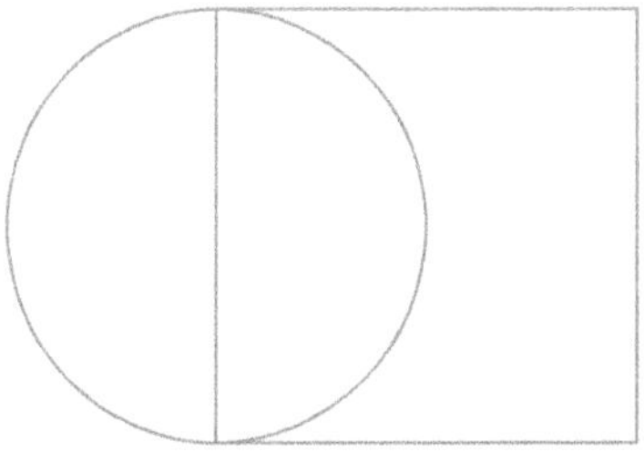

NOTES

30

Which column is greater?	
Column A	Column B
O is the center of the circle with radius = 6.	
Arc ABC	6

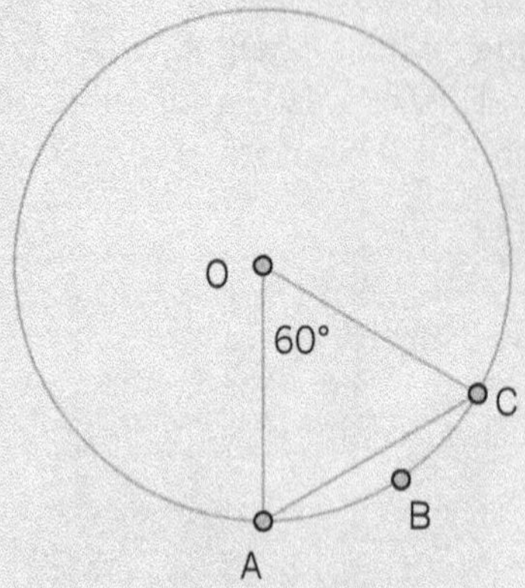

30. Column A is greater.

Triangle AOC must be equilateral since the radius of the circle is 6. Therefore, length AC = 6, and thus, the arc ABC must be greater than 6.

NOTES

PART 3

WHERE TO GO NEXT

You are now armed with understanding why routines matter and how they develop number sense and reasoning. You hopefully see how they can engage your students. You have examined a host of examples and modifications ready to implement in your classroom. So where do you go next?

MAKE A PLAN

Using routines in your mathematics classrooms might be considerably different than what you have done previously. To be successful, you need to craft a plan that addresses fundamental considerations. First, identify the mathematics concepts and content you want to focus on with your students. Next, determine which routines you think will work best. Think about a rotation of routines and whether you will change them out daily or work with one routine for a few days before moving to the next. Set goals for your work.

Identify Content for Routines

Routines are usually not intended as first instruction or reteaching of mathematics concepts. They should be opportunities for students to practice and apply the skills and concepts they have already attained. Routines should be engagement opportunities for reasoning and discussion. The skills or concepts that you select should be relative to where your students are. The intent is to advance all students' reasoning and mental mathematics abilities. You should also keep in mind that all of the routines have the flexibility to accommodate any of the skills, concepts, or numbers that you select.

Identify Routines

It's likely that every teacher has a preference for certain representations, strategies, or techniques in general. The same can probably be said about the preference of routines. A collection of routines is presented here. Some may simply be more appealing to you than others. The intent is to provide options for you rather than a sequence of routines to "cover" or "complete."

Determine the Rotation

Doing the same routine each day may become mundane quite quickly. Even if it doesn't, you might find that your students continuously employ the same types of reasoning or arguments. To avoid this, it is important to rotate the routines to keep engagement and thinking fresh.

It's important to realize that you don't have to dedicate a specific number of days or class periods per routine before rotating to another. The time spent with two different routines may not be equivalent. You can plan the amount of time you spend with a routine based on your students' needs, engagement, interest, and excitement for it. However, even if you spend a few extra days with a certain routine, you should plan to move on from it so that it doesn't become stale. You should be mindful of those routines that students truly enjoy and plan to come back to them throughout the year.

Give It Time

It's unlikely that many of your students have had many opportunities to work with activities not directly related to the concepts they are learning. Others have likely had few opportunities to engage in thinking and reasoning activities grounded in number sense and mental mathematics. That number of students probably diminishes further when you factor in opportunities for discussion and justification. Most, if not all, of your students will at some point have started a mathematics lesson that features homework review and low-level warm-up. This is uncharted waters for them.

This may be uncharted waters for you. Many teachers are trained to plan an obligatory warm-up. They are led to believe that going over homework is a mathematics constitutional right. They have not or could not think about different ways to launch a class. Your first routine or two may flop because of your and your students' unfamiliarity. That is fine. It should be expected. Be patient. The best course of action is to plan and implement a routine for a few weeks and then adjust, but not eliminate.

Set Goals

You can offset the challenges with goals, but your goals should be reasonable. At first, you might set the goal of doing a routine three times a week or mastering a specific routine over the course of 2 weeks.

You can think about setting goals for your students as well. You might want to develop their use of vocabulary. You might want them to demonstrate their ability to justify their thinking or to critique the reasoning of others. You might set goals that are content specific. You can measure those goals in all sorts of ways. One way might be to revisit a routine from early in the year with the exact same numbers or concepts and compare student performance. In other situations, it might make sense to measure growing student proficiency on a brief written assessment that measures reasoning, fluency, or number sense.

ADJUST TO THEIR ADJUSTMENTS

You naturally respond to students' thinking and reasoning. You ask questions to challenge their ideas. You push back on students' strategies. You ask them to clarify. You'll need to leverage those same teacher moves during routines. You'll also need to keep in mind that as students work with routines, they'll begin to adjust their reasoning. They may begin to favor specific strategies or approaches. When they do, you'll want to respond by changing the numbers, skills, and concepts that you feature.

FURTHER MODIFY ROUTINES

Each of the routines in this book is a creation or adaptation of activities we have used in our classrooms. They have served our students well. There are directions and procedures for implementing them, but those directions are not set in stone. In fact, many of the routines presented are variations of their first offerings. There are ideas for modifying presented throughout, but more can be changed. You should feel free to change the directions or how you present routines. Adjust them to make them your own.

DESIGN YOUR OWN ROUTINES

These routines are all built on the notions of reasoning and number sense. They all feature opportunities for students to discuss and defend their reasoning. You can modify almost any activity to become a routine. As you become more comfortable with routines, you can begin to develop your own based on games and activities you use during your instruction. You can look for other routines online. You might even investigate the routines that are available in other grade levels to consider how you might incorporate them into your own instruction.

We also suggest that you have students take the next step and create their own examples from our various routines. Bloom's revised taxonomy places *create* at the very top of the triangle.

Bloom's Taxonomy

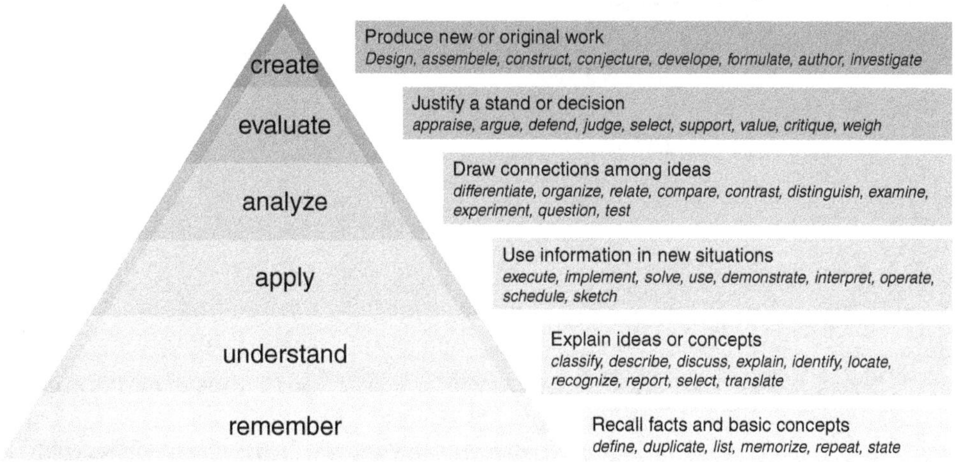

Bloom's Taxonomy. Created by @cirtlmooc http://hiscience.pbworks.com/f/1467974486/Bloomtaxonomy.jpg

When students produce new or original work, they are working at the highest cognitive process dimension.

WORK COLLABORATIVELY AND SHARE THE LOAD

Sometimes your students' creative thinking will inspire new possibilities or new routines. Keep in mind that your colleagues are also an excellent creative source for generating examples. When teachers plan together, they learn about others' perspectives, experiences, and mathematical insights. They learn about how others think and reason about numbers and computation. The exchange of ideas with your colleagues can help you reinforce and grow your own ideas. It will help you prepare. It will help you facilitate student reasoning through discussion.

Leveraging insights from other teachers and students is also a great way to share the workload. For example, four teachers on a team could each create four sets of prompts for a routine. If those four teachers share their four, each teacher would have a routine planned for 16 days, or a little more than 3 weeks. Each of those teachers could also have students create examples of their routine. If so, they could select four student examples and rotate them as well. In doing so, a teacher who created four examples could wind up with 32 days ready to go.

We want to engage with you and learn from your ideas and creations, too. We welcome your modifications and new examples of these routines, as we plan on collecting them and sharing them electronically within our community of educators. Submissions can be sent to us at https://tinyurl.com/routinesubmission.

JUMP-START MATHEMATICS ENGAGEMENT, NUMBER SENSE, AND REASONING

Starting each mathematics class with a routine is an opportunity to jump-start engagement, number sense, and reasoning. These routines are quality tasks for working with a wide range of skills and concepts. They are opportunities for promoting engagement through novel prompts, interesting situations, and discussion. They are opportunities to play with numbers. They are a chance for us to do something about the rhetorical "they just don't have number sense" or "they just don't know how to think."

REFERENCES

Boaler, J. (2015a). *Mathematical mindsets: Unleashing students' potential through creative math, inspiring messages, and innovative teaching.* San Francisco, CA: Jossey-Bass.

Boaler, J. (2015b, May 7). Memorizers are the lowest achievers and other Common Core math surprises. *Hechinger Report.* Retrieved from http://hechingerreport.org/

Dweck, C. (2006). *Mindset: The new psychology of success.* New York, NY: Penguin Random House.

Fennell, F., & Landis, T. E. (1994). Number sense and operation sense. In C. A. Thornton & N. S. Bley (Eds.), *Windows of opportunity: Mathematics for students with special needs* (pp. 187–203). Reston, VA: National Council of Teachers of Mathematics.

Gladwell, M. (2008). *Outliers: The story of success.* New York, NY: Little, Brown.

Grouws, D. A., Tarr, J. E., Sears, R., & Ross, D. J. (2010, January). *Mathematics teachers' use of instructional time and relationships to textbook content organization and class period format.* Paper presented at the Hawaii International Conference on Education, Honolulu, HI.

Kilpatrick, J., Swafford, J., & Findell, B. (Eds.). (2001). *Adding it up: Helping children learn mathematics.* Washington, DC: National Academies Press.

National Council of Teachers of Mathematics. (1989). *Curriculum and evaluation standards for school mathematics.* Reston, VA: Author.

National Council of Teachers of Mathematics. (2000). *Principles and standards for school mathematics.* Reston, VA: Author.

National Council of Teachers of Mathematics. (2014). *Principles to actions: Ensuring mathematical success for all.* Reston, VA: Author.

National Governors Association Center for Best Practices & Council of Chief State School Officers. (2010). *Common core state standards, mathematics.* Washington, DC: Author.

O'Connell, S., & SanGiovanni, J. (2013). *Putting practice into action: Implementing the common core standards for mathematical practice.* Portsmouth, NH: Heinemann.

Otten, S., Herbel-Eisenmann, B. A., & Cirillo, M. (2012, August 22). Going over homework in mathematics classrooms: An unexamined activity. *Teachers College Record.* http://www.tcrecord.org

Smith, M. S., & Stein, M. K. (2018). *5 practices for orchestrating productive mathematics discussions* (2nd ed.). Reston, VA: National Council of Teachers of Mathematics.

Sousa, D. (2007). *How the brain learns mathematics.* Thousand Oaks, CA: Corwin.

Van de Walle, J. A., Karp, K. S., & Bay-Williams, J. M. (2010). *Elementary and middle school mathematics: Teaching developmentally* (7th ed.). New York, NY: Allyn and Bacon.

NOTES

NOTES

NOTES

NOTES

NOTES

NOTES

NOTES

NOTES

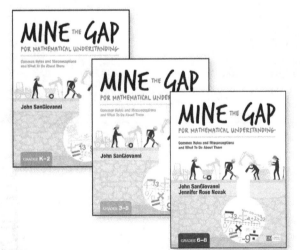

Supporting Teachers, Empowering Learners

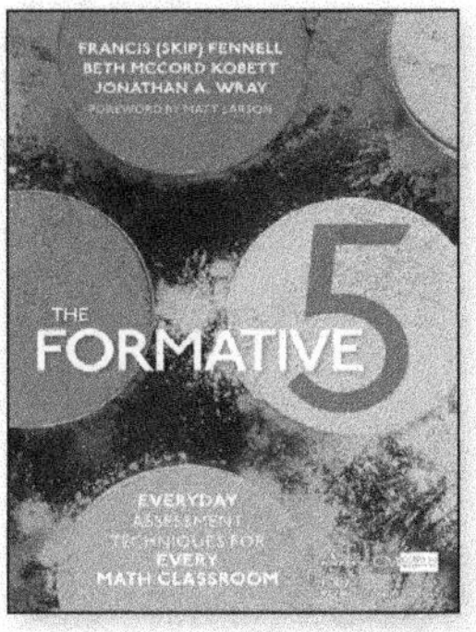

Move the needle on math instruction with these 5 assessment techniques

Francis (Skip) Fennell, Beth McCord Kobett, and Jonathan A. Wray

Grades K–8

eCourse and PD Resource Center now available!

Get them talking: Your formula for bringing math concepts to life!

Jennifer Knudsen, Harriette S. Stevens, Teresa Lara-Meloy, Hee-Joon Kim, and Nicole Shechtman

Grades 6–8

Your whole-school solution to mathematics standards

When it comes to math, standards-aligned is achievement-aligned…

Linda M. Gojak and Ruth Harbin Miles

Grades K–2

Linda M. Gojak and Ruth Harbin Miles

Grades 3–5

Ruth Harbin Miles and Lois A. Williams

Grades 6–8

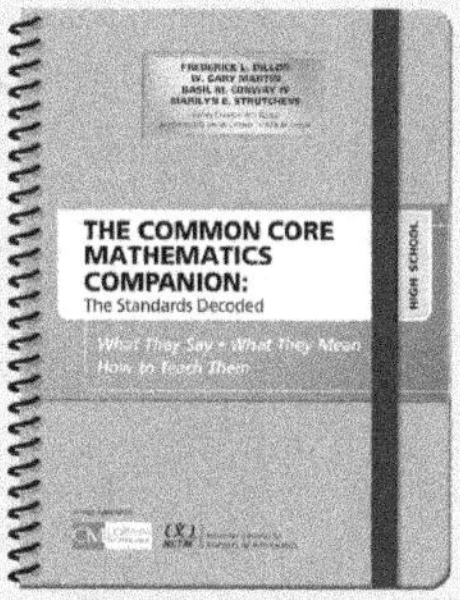

Frederick L. Dillon, W. Gary Martin, Basil M. Conway IV, and Marilyn E. Strutchens

High School

New series for states with state-specific mathematics standards

Grades K–2, Grades 3–5, Grades 6–8, High School

N187E6

CORWIN
A SAGE Publishing Company